DATE DUE			
			PRINTED IN U.S.A.

OVER
NEW ENGLAND

OVER
NEW ENGLAND

Text by Neal R. Peirce

Photography by Stephen Proehl

WELDON
OWEN

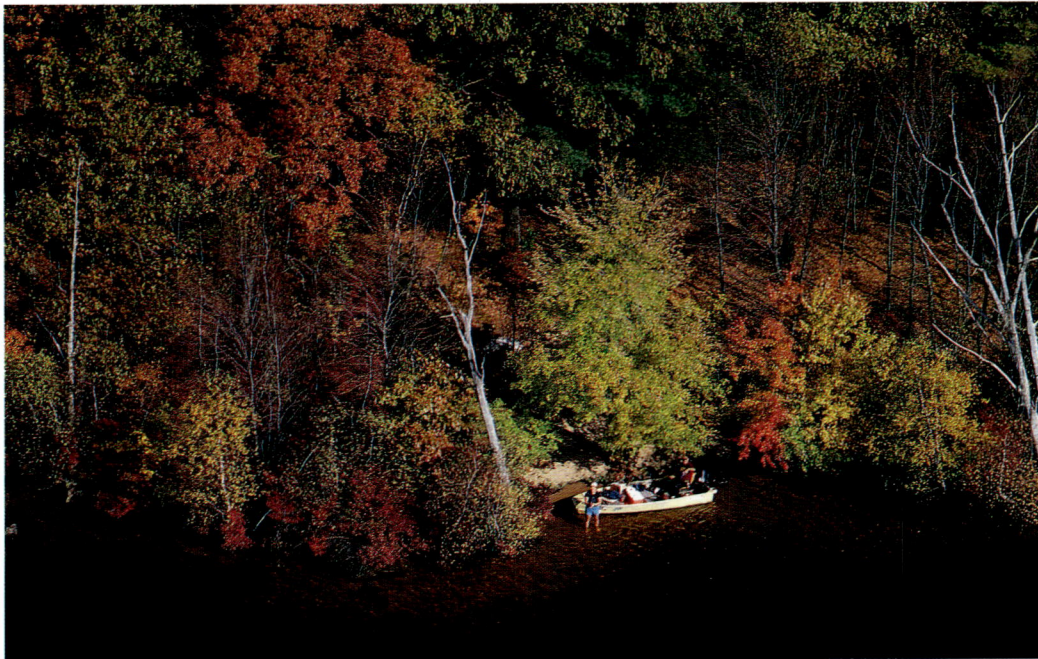

ALEX S. MACLEAN/LANDSLIDES

A WINGS OVER AMERICA® Project

Copyright © 1998 Weldon Owen Inc.
Weldon Owen Inc., 814 Montgomery Street, San Francisco, CA 94133
Telephone: (415) 291-0100 Fax: (415) 291-8841

ISBN 1-887451-21-8

WINGS OVER AMERICA® Series
President: John Owen
Associate Editor: Laurie Wertz
Copy Editor: Virginia Rich
Researcher/On-Site Location Coordinator: Barbara Roether
Design: Tom Morgan, Blue Design (from an original concept
    by John Bull, The Book Design Company)
Map: Mike Gorman
Production Director: Stephanie Sherman

OVER® NEW ENGLAND text by Neal R. Peirce
Principal photography by Stephen Proehl
Fixed wing pilots: Ron Benham, Doug Brown, Daneane Carothers,
    Keith Hasberg, Tom Martin, Chris Rathburn
Helicopter pilots: Mike Peavey, Roger Sharkey

Printed by Toppan Printing Co., China
Printed in China

Above
A day of fishing in central Connecticut.

Right
Morning in residential Bangor, Maine.

Endpapers
Windblown shoals off Chatham, Cape Cod, Massachusetts.

Page 1
A Stearman biplane cuts across the Newport coastline.

Pages 2–3
A red sea of cranberries colors a bog near Lakeville, Massachusetts.

Pages 4–5
A thriving dairy farm in Tunbridge, Vermont.

Pages 6–7
Twilight in the White Mountain foothills of New Hampshire.

Pages 8–9
A frozen creek catches the light in Packer, Connecticut.

Pages 12–13
More than 9,000 runners gather in Hopkinton, Massachusetts, for the start of
the 1990 Boston Marathon.

Page 14
Autumn comes to Acworth, New Hampshire.

Pages 16–17
A Boston cross section: John Hancock Tower, Back Bay and the Charles River.

Page 18
Tobacco fields and barns in Franklin County, Massachusetts.

Page 21
Mount Desert Island, Maine.

FOREWORD

Maine has been my life and has made my life possible for me. I was privileged to serve her as governor more than 30 years ago and to represent her in the United States Senate for more than 20 years; and all because my immigrant father chose Maine as the place to begin a new life a third of a world away from the Russian-occupied Poland where he was born. He joined Irish, Italians, French Canadians and other immigrants who enriched the earlier Yankee heritage. As the years unfolded, my roots sank deeply into the soil of a region of surpassing beauty and diversity, and a culture of increasing openness and opportunity.

These pages provide magnificent exposure to the dramatic contrasts in New England's physical attractions: Maine's vast forest-covered north country and storied rockbound coast; the natural wonders of Cape Cod; Rhode Island's shimmering Narragansett Bay; the fertile Connecticut River Valley; Vermont's gentle fields and hills; New Hampshire's rugged White Mountains; and the lake country sprinkled across the region. The images in *Over New England* provide the setting for a history that goes back to America's beginnings. It is the history of a people seeking a new world, taming a wilderness, fighting for independence, building lives and communities, creating a nation.

The Industrial Revolution, which transformed America into a mighty industrial engine, had its beginnings in New England. Over the years, the ebb and flow of economic forces has bypassed isolated rural areas and left dilapidated mill towns behind, breeding poverty and subsistence living for too many. The vitality inherent in the New England spirit has responded to these challenges and taken advantage of high-tech modernization to build more diversified, entrepreneurial economies. Similarly, early industrial growth defiled pristine streams and abused seemingly limitless natural resources. Here, too, a more enlightened age is responding with environmental policies to heal past damage and to prohibit such depredation.

On the whole, as this volume will attest, New England is alive and well. Her sons and daughters, her values, her institutions have been a vital force in our development and in the development of the country to the west of us.

There is continuing work to be done. We believe that the future should be open to each of us and that we each share in the responsibility to make it so. We are confident of our ability to move into that future, using the prudence, creativity and sense of community so typical of our people. To sustain us in that confidence, we have the home which nature has provided us and which is so inspiringly portrayed in *Over New England*.

Edmund S. Muskie
Maine State Legislature 1947–55
Governor of Maine 1955–59
Senator from Maine 1959–80
U.S. Secretary of State 1980–81

CONTENTS

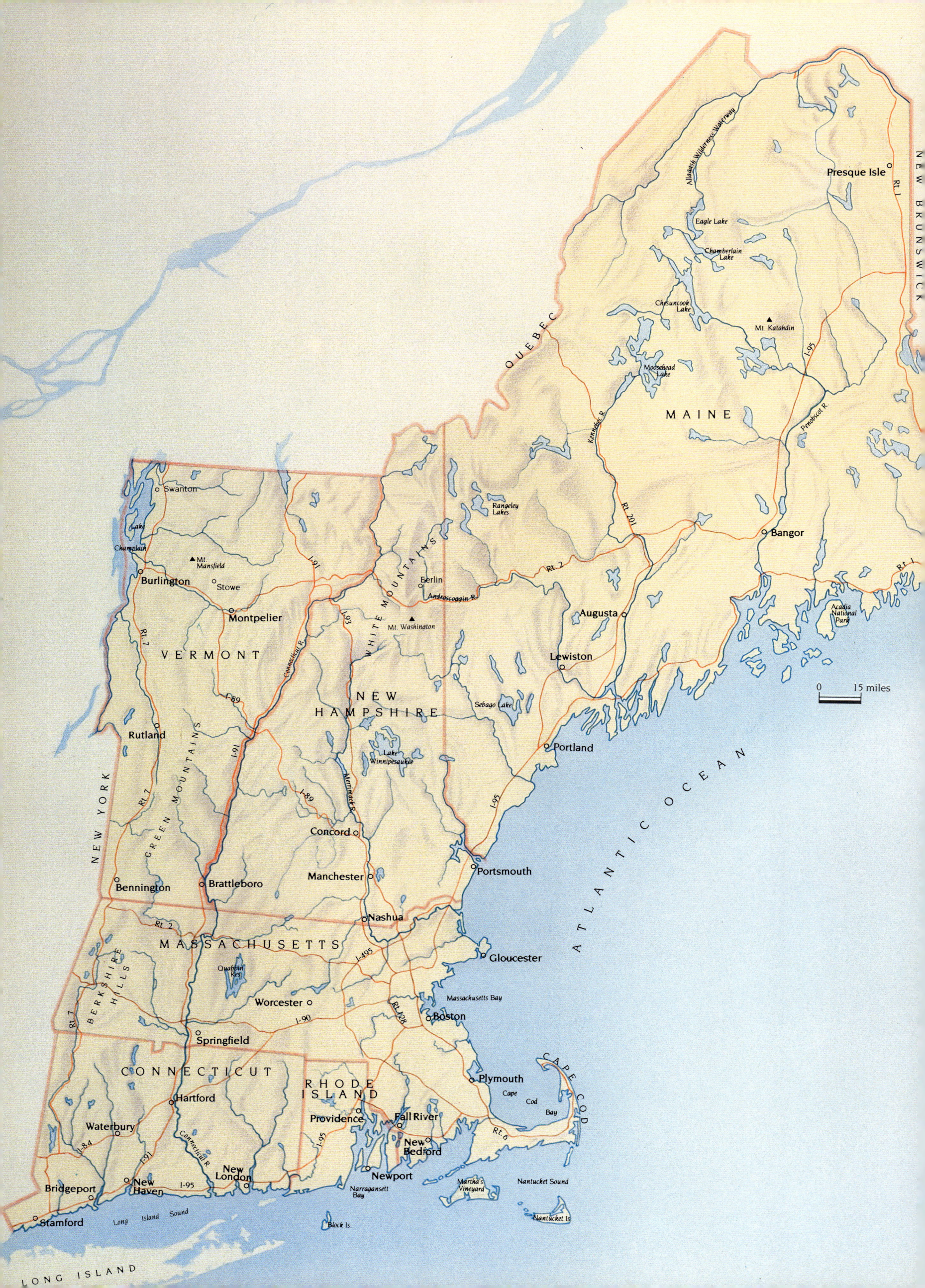

NEW BRUNSWICK

Presque Isle

Rt. 1

QUEBEC

Allagash Wilderness Waterway

Eagle Lake

Chamberlain Lake

Chesuncook Lake

Mt. Katahdin

Moosehead Lake

Kennebec R.

MAINE

Penobscot R.

Rt. 201

Rt. 2

Bangor

Rangeley Lakes

Acadia National Park

Rt. 1

Swanton

Lake Champlain

Mt Mansfield

Burlington

Stowe

Berlin

Androscoggin R.

Augusta

I-91

WHITE MOUNTAINS

Montpelier

Mt. Washington

Rt. 2

VERMONT

I-93

Lewiston

Connecticut R.

NEW HAMPSHIRE

Sebago Lake

15 miles

0

Rutland

I-89

Lake Winnipesaukee

Portland

GREEN MOUNTAINS

I-91

Merrimack R.

ATLANTIC OCEAN

Concord

I-89

NEW YORK

Rt. 7

Portsmouth

Bennington

Brattleboro

Manchester

I-95

Rt. 7

Nashua

Rt. 2

MASSACHUSETTS

Gloucester

I-495

Berkshire Hills

Quabbin Res.

Worcester

Massachusetts Bay

Rt. 128

I-90

Boston

Springfield

Rt. 7

CAPE COD

CONNECTICUT

RHODE ISLAND

Plymouth

Hartford

Cape Cod Bay

Waterbury

Providence

Fall River

Rt. 6

I-84

Connecticut R.

New Bedford

I-91

New London

Newport

I-95

Bridgeport

New Haven

Martha's Vineyard

Nantucket Sound

Stamford

Narragansett Bay

Long Island Sound

Block Is.

Nantucket Is.

LONG ISLAND

Cobscook Bay

"New England has a harsh climate, a barren soil, a rough and stormy coast, and yet we love it, even with a love passing those of dwellers in more favored regions."

The words of Henry Cabot Lodge, U.S. senator from Massachusetts in the early 1900s, resonate down through the years. The call of New England is not to sheer size and grandeur: for that try a state like Montana, alone twice New England's 66,806 square miles. Nor to fertility: up over the hills, through forests that were once open fields, you can still trace the lines of stone walls built by hardy pioneer farmers on land that was so harsh that their sons and grandsons would in time strike out for the Midwest's broader, less rocky fields. Nor does the region feature balminess: I write these words on a windy and blindingly white December morning in New Hampshire, the temperature hovering near zero Fahrenheit.

What New England is is quintessential America. Much like Old England, it was the womb of a civilization, the starting place for the colonization of vast spaces, the fountainhead of a culture's language, law and learning. It is the region whose severe Puritanism gave birth to the town meeting and the idea of local, participatory democracy in America. The early Yankees—proud, principled, taciturn, self-reliant—fostered a durable tradition of independence of mind and of nonconformity. Irish, Italians, French Canadians and other immigrants soon outnumbered the Yankees, giving New England a new, ethnically richer cast. Yet the independent early spirit endures.

Physical New England encompasses many worlds, from the turbulent sea off the Maine coast to the quiet Connecticut shores on Long Island Sound, from the lush Connecticut River Valley to the granite, storm-thrashed summit of Mount Washington, from late twentieth-century suburban tracts and office parks to the largely unpeopled expanses of the "north country." Church-steeple-village New England lives on. But here too is a region of gritty industrial towns, high-tech corridors, skyscraper cities, neighborhoods both affluent and devastatingly poor, and cheap sprawl development which engulfs little towns and threatens to devour the spaces between New England's very special places.

In these pages the camera's eye sweeps in over the dramatic sea- and mountainscape of Maine, through the region's lead state and economic capital of Massachusetts, over scrappy little Rhode Island. Then it's on to semimetropolitan Connecticut (half suburb, half village), up over picturesque Vermont, and a finale viewing of New Hampshire, the Granite State. Independent, politically and culturally variegated, the six states share and encapsulate all that *is* New England, past and present.

NORTHERN LIGHT

MAINE

Long Lake
Square Lake
Eagle Lake
St. John R.
Allagash R.
Caribou
Rt. 11
Presque Isle
Rt. 1

Eagle Lake
Millinocket Lake
Chamberlain Lake
Grand Lake Matagamon
Baxter State Park
Chesuncook Lake
Mt. Katahdin
I-95
Houlton
Sherman Mills

Moosehead Lake
Millinocket Lake
Millinocket
Baskahegan Lake
Greenville
Penobscot R.

Rt. 201
Flagstaff Lake
Sebec Lake
Sebec R.
Piscataquis R.
Grand Falls
West Grand Lake
Big Lake
St. Croix R.

Rangeley Lake
Sugarloaf Mtn.
Dexter
Rt. 9
Eastport
Campobello Is.
Bay of Fundy
Mooselookmeguntic Lake
Kennebec R.
Skowhegan
Bangor
Cobscook Bay
West Quoddy Head

Rumford
Rt. 2
Waterville
Graham Lake
Machias
Rt.
Androscoggin R.
Jonesport

Fryeburg
Castine
Blue Hill
Acadia National Park
0   20 miles
Augusta
Camden
Rt. 26
Lewiston
Thompson Lake
Long Lake
Dresden Mills
Rockland
Penobscot Bay
Wiscasset
Vinalhaven Is.
Damariscotta
Sebago Lake
Freeport
Bath
I-95
Boothbay Harbor
Pemaquid Point
Portland
Cape Elizabeth
Kennebunkport

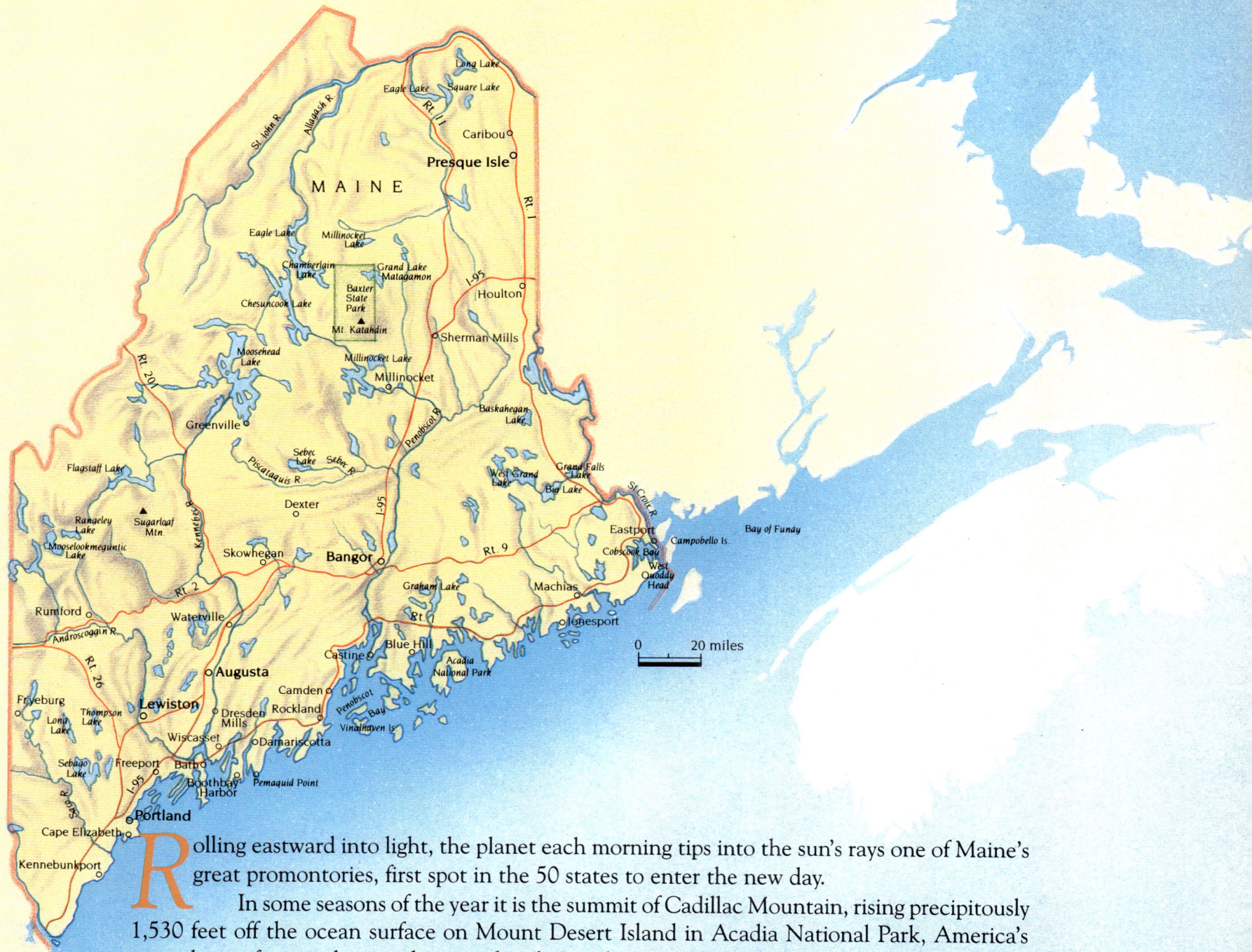

Rolling eastward into light, the planet each morning tips into the sun's rays one of Maine's great promontories, first spot in the 50 states to enter the new day.

In some seasons of the year it is the summit of Cadillac Mountain, rising precipitously 1,530 feet off the ocean surface on Mount Desert Island in Acadia National Park, America's second most frequently visited national park. In other seasons the sun first strikes West Quoddy Head, the nation's most easterly point, where the Coast Guard maintains a famous candy-striped lighthouse that dates from 1807. Here the tides range from 24 to 28 feet, the nation's highest, and spruce and fir stand sentinel on the ridge lines of once-lofty mountains.

All the Maine coast, with its seeming infinity of bays, inlets, harbors and some 1,200 islands surrounded by dangerous reefs and shoals, is in fact a great drowned mountain range, pressed deep into the earth's crust by the massive glaciers that advanced from the polar cap starting some million years ago. The last receded only 12,000 years past.

Near Quoddy Head is Campobello Island, where the Roosevelt Campobello International Park, commemorating international peace and goodwill between the United States and Canada, was dedicated in 1964. Here Franklin Roosevelt spent his youthful summers and respites through a long career.

And a hundred miles inland, above a vast wilderness, soars that great monarch in granite, Mount Katahdin (5,267 feet), Maine's highest peak. Katahdin is northern anchor of the 2,000-mile-long Appalachian Trail, the continuous footpath which ends at Springer Mountain, Georgia. In some seasons Katahdin's peak is also first in America to welcome the sun—six hours before solar rays filter onto the slopes of fiery Mauna Loa and Mauna Kea on Hawaii's Big Island.

Left: Portland Head Light has protected ships from the rocky shores of Cape Elizabeth since George Washington ordered its construction in 1790. *Previous pages:* Rosy dawn illuminates Mount Desert Island.

25

Above: Forests climb to the precipitous edge of Ironbound Island near Acadia National Park. *Right:* Inland, the violent clash of land and sea gives way to a broad-reaching wilderness of forests, bogs and uncharted streams, like this one near Moosehead Lake.

Maine is a state of American beginnings, from the first Viking ships in the eleventh century to Captain John Smith, who visited the coast from Penobscot down to Cape Cod in 1614, making a map of the territory he named "New England." Smith wrote of coves and inlets without number "where you may take many clams or lobsters or both at your pleasure," the rockbound coast bordering "good woods for building houses, boats, barks and ships. . . ."

Its picturesque historic fishing and vacation towns hugging the granite-ledged shoreline, Maine has one of the world's most painted, photographed, written-about coasts. Artists and artisans, antique shop entre-

preneurs, tourists and fugitives from urban America crowd such towns as Camden, Rockland, Rockport and York Village.

But "quaint" Maine is a faulty vision. There's little charm in the less attractive strip development in southern Maine, or in the garish development blighting some of the tourist traps along the hundreds of miles of coastal Route 1. The posh exurbanite lifestyle is a foreign concept to a county like Washington, northeasterly along the coast, where communities remain isolated, incomes are low, medical services few, and subsistence living some of the toughest on the North American continent. Maine's per capita income and living standards trail far behind New England averages; indeed they rank among America's lowest outside Appalachia and the Deep South.

A continental cul-de-sac (it touches only New Hampshire), Maine is, by regional standards, quite vast—almost as large as New England's other five states combined. Aroostook, the great potato county to the north, is bigger than all of Connecticut and Rhode Island. Vast stretches of the state are covered by forested "wild lands," outside any municipality. Most are owned by huge paper companies, semi-sovereignties within the great sovereignty of Maine.

Maine is a demanding, rigorous place to live. Great "Nor'easters" sweep in from land and sea. Epic fogs roll in from the Bay of Fundy, lingering for days. Winters are long and hard. Lumbermen labor in isolated camps, battling ice and snow in winter season, vicious black flies come spring. Lobstermen, out on the rugged bays and inlets up to twelve hours a day, must cope with the eternal factors of the sea, the weather, the vagaries of the catch. The traditional top Maine industries—leather (shoes), paper, lumber, shipbuilding, food processing, textiles—have been (with the sole exception of shipbuilding) low-wage, high-polluting enterprises.

With increasing courage, the state has cracked down on pulp mills and other onetime gross polluters of its pristine, free-flowing rivers and has resisted proposals for massive but environmentally hazardous dams and coastal oil-processing facilities. Some of the

Above: Commercial Street along the Portland waterfront is a nexus of activity in Maine's largest city. The condos that now line Central Wharf mark a gradual departure from the seafaring industries on which the city was founded.
Right: The soft pastel colors of Wiscasset suit the town where American ice cream was invented.

environmental choices have been difficult—local industrial jobs vs. tourism, for example, or fast forest exploitation vs. saving and replanting trees for long-term conservation. But Maine seems on a clear pro-environment track and is even starting to insist that towns enforce rigorous land-use standards to save the special Maine environment and character.

Recent years have brought high-tech and big-time retailing (L.L. Bean and others) and such a diversified, entrepreneurial economy to the Portland area that one out of four persons working there has a managerial or professional position. With telecommunications, even rural Maine's isolation is cracking, and towns with well-educated workforces are posi-

tioned to compete in the new global economy. The manufacturing base is spreading and democratizing, with many smaller firms making their mark with programmable, computer-driven machinery, networking among themselves.

Portland is exemplary among America's small cities: a town that emerged from decades of decline and a bout with destructive urban renewal to treasure its historic past, diversify its economy, draw a new generation of entrepreneurial young professionals and become a splendidly livable place. In law, finance, medicine and the arts, it outshines all other Maine towns. Revived areas like the old Port Exchange and Congress Street are now among New England's most

trendy and thriving. Yet success has brought conflict: how to maintain Portland's historic but gritty old waterfront economy of fishing and boat-making in the face of waves of development? The city's answer: a moratorium on condos.

Renewal has come belatedly, and far more tentatively, to Bangor, the "metropolis" for virtually all of northern Maine; to Augusta, the state capital; and to such older shoe or textile mill towns as Lewiston and Auburn. As for smaller towns, they have benefited from "negative preservation"—such a lack of twentieth-century economic force that they appear today much as they did in the 1920s and 1930s, from their main squares, grange halls and hardware stores to churches and adjacent farmlands.

And every newfangled sign of "progress" notwithstanding, the frugal "Down-easter" character traits live on. By its code, the frugal Yankee keeps his feelings to himself, holds back commitment, wastes few words. Yet when his neighbor is in trouble, he's instantly on tap. A frugal spirit? Perhaps. But call it an honest, trustworthy spirit, too. In a nation afflicted with slick commercialism, it's as refreshing as a sea breeze zipping across an exquisite Maine harbor on a sultry July afternoon.

Left: Bangor stands beneath a lonely church spire on the banks of the Penobscot River. Ships' masts and other lumber products made Bangor a bustling boom town in the 1850s. *Above*: A windjammer sails off the coast of Vinalhaven Island.

31

Left: The pink granite slopes of Acadia
National Park drape the Atlantic horizon
in northern Maine. The Abenaki Indians
called this place Pemetic ("the sloping
land"). When Samuel de Champlain sailed
by in 1604 he called it l'Isle des monts
deserts (' island of bare mountains").
Hundreds of bird species, rare plants and
solitary humans find the landscape to their
liking. *Above*: The meandering character of
Maine's coastline is repeated in the lake
region near Baxter State Park.

Following pages: Miles from any named
place, White Mountain foothills drift
across western Maine's remote borderlands
near Quebec, Canada.

Remote passageways bisect and intermingle in northern Maine. Buried beneath a sea of trees, I-95 cuts a beeline to Sherman Mills, gateway to the 200,000-acre wilderness of Baxter State Park. Here rivers flow unimpeded through forests of balsam fir and red spruce. It is the land of the lone canoeist and of hikers who come via the Appalachian Trail.

Right: After summer visitors leave the north woods, ski areas like 4,237-foot Sugarloaf Mountain near Rangeley Lake stay busy through the winter.

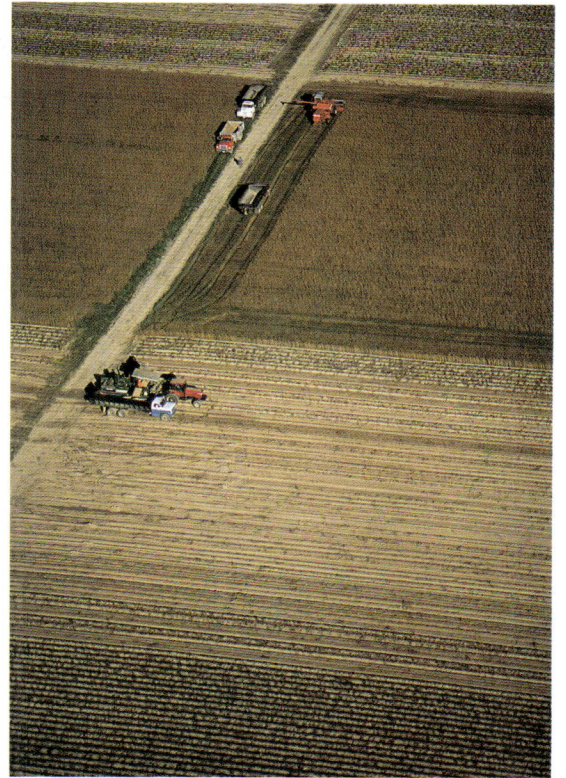

Over a million tons of potatoes are harvested each year in the fertile plains of Aroostook County in the north. Until 1989 area schoolchildren were excused from classes to work the harvest. Shipped from the northern ports of Presque Isle and Caribou, potatoes are Maine's major agricultural crop.

Previous pages: The Blue Hill Fair is typical of the county fairs held throughout New England each autumn. Along with the gaudy carnival midway, one can find such country standards as sheepdog trials, calf judging, tractor pulls and blueberry pie bake-offs.

Another link in the unfolding scenery
of coastal Route 1, the idyllic town of
Damariscotta lies along the tidal river that
shares its name.

The smokestacks of the Great Northern paper mill in Millinocket have been a fixture on the landscape since 1900. Turning the Maine woods into newsprint for papers such as the *Boston Globe* is a thriving business: Great Northern is the largest landowner in the state and employs several thousand people. Fueled in part by hydroelectric power from the West Branch of the Penobscot River, the mills here produce over 2,000 tons of paper each day.

*E*leven thousand people are employed by the Bath Iron Works, where these steel frames will become carriers and destroyers for the U.S. Navy. Though ship design has changed radically in 250 years, Maine's preoccupation with building them has not. The first shipyards at Bath opened in 1762. By the late 1800s the town's wooden schooners were among the finest on the seas. Local iron foundries helped Bath lead the way in construction of modern steel ships, and today the launch of a new vessel still draws a crowd.

Right: The dying crimson vines of wild blueberries color the ground for miles around a lone house near Addison. The blueberry, canned and frozen, is a major cash crop in Washington County.
Below: Peat bogs like this one on Louds Island are common in low-lying areas; the subtle olive-colored moss is prized by florists.

*B*oaters follow the coiling path of the Songo River as it nears Songo Locks. Despite obvious difficulties, lumber freighters once navigated the river, which links Sebago Lake with Long Lake, through Songo Locks.

Chances are the lobster you eat in Chicago came from Rockland, a bustling fishing town on Penobscot Bay. Three-quarters of the national supply comes from Maine, and Rockland is the largest exporter of lobster in the world. Caught in baited traps, or pots, set on the bottom of relatively shallow bays and harbors, the size and number of the lobster catch has declined dramatically in recent years. Three- or four-pound lobsters were once common; today five inches, 1¼ pounds is standard.

South of Augusta, a tiny farm hugs the winding shore of the Eastern River. Small mill towns like nearby Dresden Mills were common along the rivers of the southern interior in the nineteenth century. Such towns have now almost disappeared, swallowed into the larger industrial centers of Lewiston and Augusta, while the land has retained its rural character.

Double bridges cast their shadows on the frozen Penobscot River in Bangor. The town was once a major exporter of ice. Cut from the area's many lakes and rivers, ice was free for the taking and fetched a handsome price along the sweltering banks of the Ganges.

The commercial center of northern Maine, Bangor still retains its frontier quality. The ice rink cleared from the snowy town square is not for export but for skating and hockey practice.

Above: President George Bush's grand-parents built this 26-room house on the tip of a secluded peninsula near Kennebunkport on the southern coast. Used as a summer White House, the "cottage" is kept intentionally undecorated to retain the rustic Maine atmosphere.

Right: Similiar in setting if not in mood, Fort Popham guards the entrance to the Kennebec River. Built in 1861 at the start of the Civil War, the 30-foot-thick granite walls were never put to test in battle.

Opposite: The Bushes' summer neighbors find room for more than one cottage on their own nearby peninsula, Lord's Point. The area's native patriotism is evidenced by the flag flying on the lawn.

"Down-easters" celebrate their seafaring spirit in the annual windjammer festival at Boothbay Harbor (above). Sailing ships are a particular pride in Maine. The clipper ship *Red Jacket*, built in Rockland in 1854, was once the fastest ship to sail across the Atlantic. The *Ranger*, built in Bath, won the America's Cup in 1937. Returning from Vinalhaven Island under full sail, modern windjammers (opposite) carry the tradition into the twenty-first century.

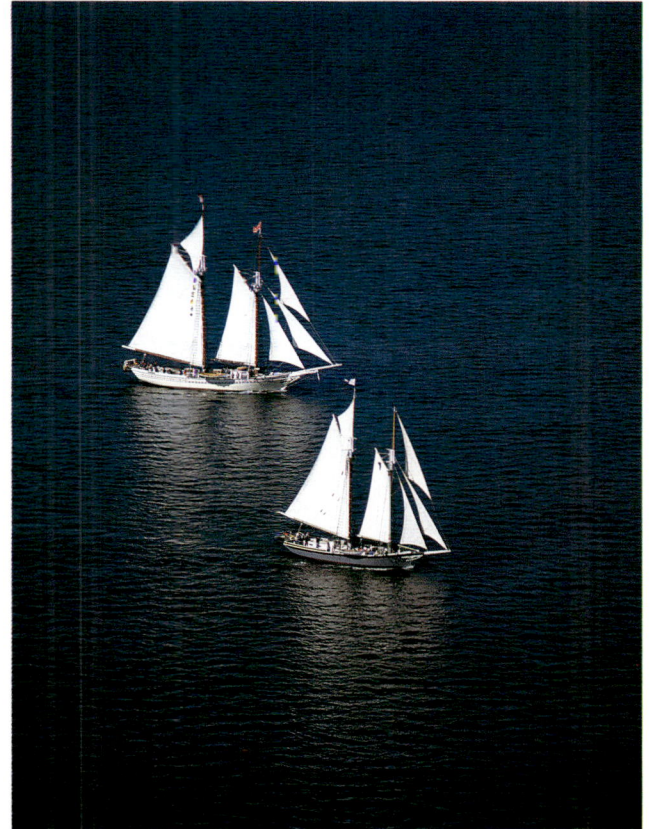

Salmon nurseries float on the cool waters of Cobscook Bay on Maine's eastern border near New Brunswick, Canada. Nearby Eastport, a large fish-canning center, manufactures an essence from ground fish scales that is used to give artificial pearls their iridescent shine.

*B*ustins Island *(foreground)* in Maquoit
Bay is often welded to the mainland by a
heavy sheet of ice during the winter
months. This area, near Freeport, falls on
a Maine "weather line." To the north,
the uneven coast is often iced in for the
winter, and temperatures dip below zero
at least ten days a year. To the south,
slightly milder conditions prevail.

*C*oastal weather is mild compared
to the snowfalls and temperatures
imposed on mountainous areas such as
Rangeley Lakes, though a golden
sunset can warm even the coldest day.

LANDFALL

Williamstown • Rt. 7 • Hoosic R. • Rt. 2 • Deerfield R. • Millers R. • Greenfield • Fitchburg • Rt. 2 • Groton • Lowell • I-95 • Ipswich • Haverhill • Newburyport • Plum Is. • Merrimack R. • CAPE ANN • Gloucester • Manchester • Salem • Massachusetts Bay

MASSACHUSETTS • Leominster • Nashua R. • Concord R. • Rt. 128 • I-93 • Cambridge • BERKSHIRE HILLS • Pittsfield • Hatfield • Amherst • Quabbin Res. • Ware R. • Wachusett Res. • Marlborough • Assabet R. • Concord • Lexington • Charles R. • Boston • Quincy

Littleville Lake • Stockbridge • I-90 • Holyoke • Connecticut R. • Brookfield • Worcester • Rt. 9 • Framingham • I-90 • I-495 • Walpole • Rt. 3

Cobble Mtn. Res. • Agawam • Springfield • Westfield R. • Wallum R. • Sturbridge • Southbridge • I-395 • I-90 • Brockton • Rt. 24 • Plymouth • Plymouth Bay

CAPE COD • Provincetown • Cape Cod National • Attleboro • Taunton • Lakeville • I-495 • Cape Cod Bay • Sandwich • Barnstable • Yarmouth • Chatham • Rt. 6 • Fall River • I-195 • New Bedford • Falmouth • Nantucket Sound • Buzzards Bay • Elizabeth Is. • Vineyard Sound • Martha's Vineyard • Nantucket Is.

0 10 miles

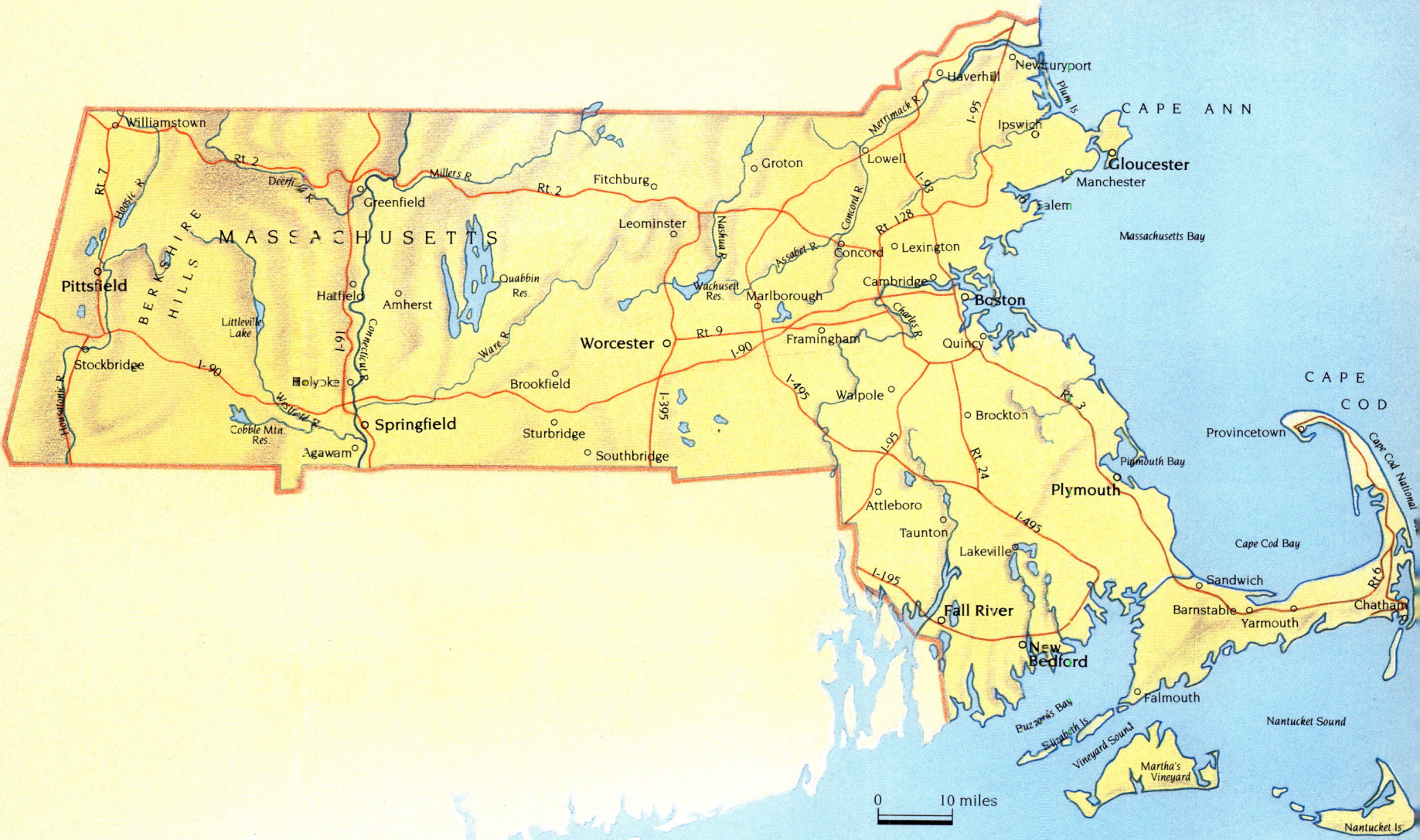

Historic icons, many of them revered touchstones of the American Revolution, crowd into central Boston. In their numbers they suggest a museum of a nation's birthing and New England heritage. Yet they are not alone: they stand among a virtual forest of modern skyscrapers. Beside fragile eighteenth-century structures soar the towers in which the corporate governance, the financial management of New England's vibrant lead city, takes place.

One could speak of the modern office towers, new sentinels of the Massachusetts skyline. But against history, they are dull stuff. Far better to tell of Faneuil Hall, the "Cradle of Liberty" where Samuel Adams, James Otis and others delivered the fiery speeches that would lead to the American Revolution. Or how up Tremont Street one comes upon the Old Granary Burying Ground, the great posthumous gathering place of such Revolutionary heroes as John Hancock, Samuel Adams, Peter Faneuil and Paul Revere. Or to recall how the pedestrian, within minutes, will stumble upon such treasures as the Boston Atheneum, literary *sanctum sanctorum* of Old Boston; King's Chapel, once Anglican Church for loyalists, later America's first Unitarian church; the Old South Meeting House where Bostonians met to protest the British tea tax before their famous Tea Party; the Old State House; the scene of the Boston Massacre; the Paul Revere House; and the Old North Church immortalized in Longfellow's poem about Revere's midnight ride ("One if by land and two if by sea").

Sloping up Beacon Hill is the green expanse of the Boston Common, land the town bought in the 1600s as a "trayning field" for militia, plus "feeding of Cattell"—acres where pirates, witches and Quakers were hanged from an elm tree near Frog Pond. Atop the hill stands the gold-domed State House, designed by Charles Bulfinch in 1795, and close by, such cobblestoned treasures as old Acorn Street and Louisburg Square.

Left: Decked out for the Fourth of July, the USS *Constitution* circles Boston Harbor. Fondly referred to as Old Ironsides, the ship gained fame in the War of 1812 when British cannonballs bounced off her heavy oaken hull. *Previous pages:* A freighter sails from Boston out to sea.

Above: A 220-foot obelisk commemorates the 1775 Battle of Bunker Hill in Charlestown. *Right:* A photo-montage of Boston is reflected in the 10,344 panes of glass on John Hancock Tower. Some have popped loose on occasion, with (as yet) no damage to pedestrians 60 stories below.

Besides San Francisco, Boston may be America's most walkable city. And what's not quickly walkable is still not far: Bunker Hill and its obelisk marking the site of one of the Revolutionary War's most heroic engagements, for example. Or the Charlestown Navy Yard, where the old frigate *Constitution* rests, or Back Bay's gracious streets and bustling urbanism. Nearby suburbs bear such hallowed names as Lexington and Concord.

Troubling questions arose about Boston and all of Massachusetts in the years after World War II. Could this civilization survive the flight of textile and shoe firms? What about encrusted old Boston wealth: could it ever be tapped for critical modern investments? Would the social fabric be torn asunder by struggles between the Old Yankees and the Irish, or later, whites and blacks? Would the great universities in Cambridge molder on their laurels or move to reinvigorate New England's economy and intellectual life? Would dilapidated old mill towns ever revive? Would too many of Massachusetts's people head off for the Pacific Coast or the Sunbelt, leaving the state weak and exposed? Could corrupt behavior be purged from public life?

None of the worst fears were to come true. Recurrent recessions, state fiscal crises and a thousand and one political quarrels notwithstanding, Massachusetts has in fact experienced a golden age in the last half of the twentieth century. Sparked by a few farsighted leaders and the inventive genius of university faculties, the commonwealth (as it's called) got a spectacular head start in the high-technology

Left: According to Herman Melville, the "brave houses" in the old whaling town of New Bedford were "harpooned and dragged up hither from the bottom of the sea." *Above:* Harvard University found its earthly origins on the spacious plain of New Towne, a farming hamlet later renamed Cambridge.

age. The new economy created in the laboratories and factories around Boston's Route 128 loop road created immense new wealth. High-tech has been as vital to twentieth-century Massachusetts as was, in earlier times, the state's bravado and success in sending clipper ships racing about the world, in developing the maritime insurance industry, or in sparking the Industrial Revolution in the New World.

Modern Boston has been afflicted by serious racial tensions clear into the 1990s. But the fabled Yankee-Irish ethnic struggle, in which the Irish claimed their rivals were so snooty that "the Lowells talk to the Cabots, and the Cabots talk only to God," receded dramatically after World War II. An Irish-American Bay State man, John F. Kennedy, became America's first Roman Catholic president. Intermar-

riage helped a lot, too, blurring the lines between not just Yankees and Irish but Italians, Poles, Lithuanians, Portuguese and other hyphenated Americans of one of the nation's most heavily ethnic states. Indeed, Massachusetts's most interesting new class was ethnically neutral: the managers and technocrats of the post–World War II society, among them highly educated and professional administrators, teachers, lawyers, clergymen, technicians, and advertising and communications specialists.

Between the ethnic groups and the manager-technocrats, Massachusetts had the population ingredients to become one of America's most politically progressive states. Among its innovations were the nation's first "no-fault" insurance law, multiple environmental statutes, an early consumer "bill of rights," a pioneering public-school racial imbalance law, and the nation's first serious program to help welfare recipients make a smooth transition to the world of work. But by 1990 a state fiscal emergency had darkened the future for a universal health care bill passed in 1987.

The 1970s and 1980s brought stunning revival to a number of Massachusetts's old industrial cities, among them New Bedford, Worcester, Fall River and Springfield. Perhaps most dramatic of all was the turnaround of Lowell, a mill town that had been America's premier industrial city before the Civil War. By 1970, the city had deteriorated to a blighted remnant of its once-proud self. Then local civic leaders began to urge that the old mills, long despised as grimy relics of yesteryear, be recognized as architectural gems and recycled for museums, apartment houses and new industrial locations. The 5.6-mile network of stone-walled canals, gatehouses and locks was restored. A national historic park and a state heritage park were established. A large computer firm, Wang Laboratories, was persuaded to move its world headquarters into the city. Citizens began to take pride in their history and multiple ethnic backgrounds. And Lowell became world renowned as a symbol of the potential of urban revitalization.

Most famous of all Massachusetts's landmarks is Cape Cod, product of the glacier, a low-slung spit of sand and pine hooking far out into the Atlantic. Here are such protected wonders as the Cape Cod National Seashore, 30 miles from Provincetown to the ocean side of the Cape. The alarming news is the severe overuse of this premier American vacation resort. Nowhere did the tidal wave of growth engulfing New England in the 1980s throw a higher spray than along Cape Cod's highways. Retirees, telecommuters, New York's monied, assorted dealmakers and pleasure seekers of every stripe—even European and Middle Eastern investors—all rushed in. The natural Cape Cod of salt marshes, woods and hidden ponds, of quiet harbors and land-hugging bungalows, began to recede rapidly before an avalanche of shopping malls, condominiums, tacky strip development and

fearsome traffic. A slow-growth, controlled-growth movement began—belatedly—to gain strength late in the decade.

Miles out to sea from the Cape lie two more vacationers' dreams, the islands of Nantucket and Martha's Vineyard, also victims of severe modern growth pressure.

Some 70 miles west of Boston and its expanding suburban ring lies the fertile valley of the Connecticut River, the rural stretches offering rich harvests of tobacco, onions and potatoes. Reduced to minor proportions through most of the twentieth century, Massachusetts agriculture began to get positive state encouragement and grow again in the 1980s.

Still farther west rise the Berkshire Hills, whose little "hill towns" are known for their beauty and cool year-round weather. Most charming of the old Berkshire resorts is Lenox, a place rich with memories of the days when writers such as Nathaniel Hawthorne and Henry Ward Beecher lived or visited there. Lenox's Tanglewood Estate, home to the Boston Symphony's summertime concerts, has been aptly called the pastoral music capital of the United States.

Cradle of liberty, intellectual mecca, ethnic and racial tinderbox, high-technology wonder—Massachusetts has been many things to America over the centuries. History shows a state constantly surviving challenge and difficulty. The formula, inevitably, embodies the imagination, pluck and verve of the shrewd Yankee.

With fall approaching, a farmer cuts the final crop of hay from a field near Amherst.

Some few towns excepted, we are tillers of the earth, from Nova Scotia to West Florida. We are a people of cultivators, scattered over an immense territory, communicating with each other by means of good roads and navigable rivers, united by the silken bands of mild government. . . .

—Jean de Crèvecoeur, *Letters from an American Farmer*

*B*oston, the hub of New England, stands poised on the brink of the twenty-first century. Looking north, the spokes of its motions are clear. The skyscrapers of downtown, most built since 1960, shelter an older city of red brick and gardens. I-93 skirts the eastern edge of downtown, isolating the old North End. The Charles River runs inland, separating Cambridge from Boston. Due north is Charlestown, where the British parked their warships in 1775. Past Charlestown, the Mystic River flows northwest toward Lexington.

*H*ighland Light on Cape Cod has sent its beacon over the Atlantic since 1795. One of the most powerful lights on the East Coast, it can be seen by ships 45 miles distant.

The gold dome of Charles Bulfinch's masterpiece, the State House, dominates Boston's Beacon Hill. Samuel Adams and Paul Revere laid the cornerstone in 1795. Additions such as the flanking wings, built during World War I, have dramatically changed the building's appearance.

Modern renovations on Boston's waterfront include such slick additions as the Boston Harbor Hotel and office complexes on Rowe's Wharf. A crowd gathers (lower left) to wait for the ferry to Logan International Airport across the harbor. Few cities can offer travelers as grand an entryway as this heroic arch leading to Atlantic Avenue.

A patchwork crowd of Bostonians gathers to hear a Boston Pops concert on the Charles River Esplanade. Free classical music concerts are a favored Boston tradition. Ralph Waldo Emerson might have foreseen such events when he called Boston "the Athens of America."

Mt. Auburn Cemetery in Cambridge is a garden for the departed, among whom are Henry Wadsworth Longfellow and Oliver Wendell Holmes.

*B*oston's answer to Silicon Valley is "High-Tech Highway," a sprawling stretch of high-tech industries along Route 128. Electronics giants such as Honeywell, Digital, Raytheon and Wang have headquarters here. They are in a sense indigenous industries; the digital computer was created at Harvard in 1944.

Cape Cod, known for its "Cape house" architecture, has recently added tract development to its scenery. Attracted by the area's unique way of life, visitors are coming to buy. But the sight of 75 swimming pools is alarming to locals concerned about the Cape's limited supply of fresh water.

The Boston Red Sox have been playing baseball at Fenway Park since it opened in 1912. Loyal fans don't seem to mind that the Bo'sox haven't won a World Series since 1918, when a young pitcher named Babe Ruth led the team to victory. Today they're playing the Milwaukee Brewers. The Green Monster looms in left field; anything can happen.

Two small baseball diamonds break the
bleak monotony of the Massachusetts
State Penitentiary in Walpole. The
Puritan forefathers preferred to use public
humiliation rather than imprisonment;
stocks and other disciplinary implements
were common in Plymouth.

Thoreau's words about Walden Pond echo in the waters of Assawompset Pond near Lakeville:

This small lake was of most value as a neighbor in the intervals of a gentle rain storm in August, when both air and water being perfectly still, but the sky overcast, mid-afternoon had all the serenity of evening, and the wood thrush sang around, and was heard from shore to shore. . . . It is well to have some water in your neighborhood to give buoyancy to and float the earth. . . . This is as important as that it keeps butter cool.

—Henry David Thoreau, *Walden*

Though only a small proportion of New England land is now devoted to farming, a great deal is reserved for the pursuit of country pleasures. Here the Lakeville Hunt Club practices maneuvers on the broad meadows, cultivated for that purpose.

The pristine village of Hatfield (*right*) stands on the banks of the Connecticut River. The settlers who came to farm these fertile lands in the seventeenth century left the name Pioneer Valley. The Nipmuck Indians were set against losing the lush valley, and the town witnessed some of the worst Indian fights in Massachusetts history.

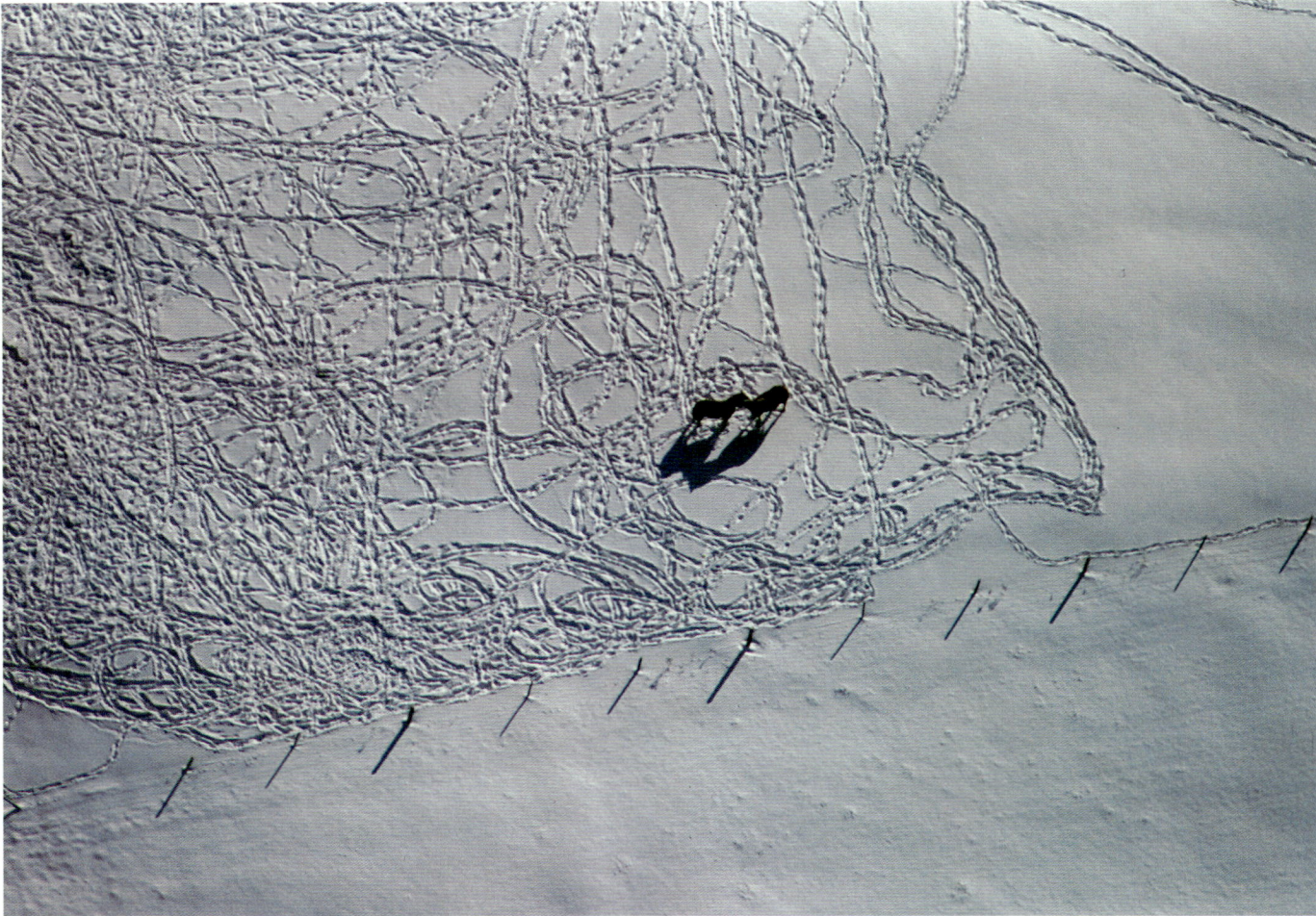

*T*wo horses pause for a short conversation about the weather behind a rambling estate in Groton. Though one might expect the owners to be old Yankees, this colonial property belongs to rock star J. Geils.

*F*or many Americans, New England is a storybook land of gentle snowfalls and sleigh rides, potbellied stoves and swimming holes. It is a story that can be bought, acre by acre, room by room. A well-preserved colonial farm like this one might be had for around half a million.

An algae-covered marsh near Stockbridge (*above*) alludes to the low-lying boggy character of much of New England. Such bogs are put to use in the cranberry industry, a $120-million annual business centered in Plymouth County (*right*). Set off by the blaze of autumn foliage, nearly 12,000 acres are harvested each year. When the scarlet berries are ripe, the bogs are flooded and the berries picked from the vine by a sort of floating thresher. Most of them become Cranberry Juice Cocktail, cranberry relish or a host of new products developed by Oceanspray Corporation, the area's major buyer-grower.

*J*ohn Hays Hammond Jr., an eccentric inventor of radio and TV components, built Hammond Castle on a rocky bluff overlooking the sea in Gloucester. Completed in 1929, the medieval fortress features secret passageways, a Roman bath, and a giant pipe organ that is still played for visitors.

*P*lumbing fixtures were the stock-in-trade of Richard Crane, who built his house, Castle Hill, near the beach in Ipswich. The Devil, in the guise of Jack Nicholson, temporarily took over the house to film the 1987 movie *The Witches of Eastwick.*

*B*athed in the mercurial rays of a winter sun, Route 128, the major expressway around Boston, leads early commuters home. A workforce of 330,000 people enter Boston each morning and leave each night for homes in neighboring towns. Among them are some 40,000 scientists and engineers drawn by jobs in the computer industry and at research facilities such as MIT.

*S*ummer revelers travel the ups and downs of the old rollercoaster at Riverside Park in Agawam. It's a welcome diversion in the Springfield area, where relatively few tourists wander, despite such attractions as the Basketball Hall of Fame.

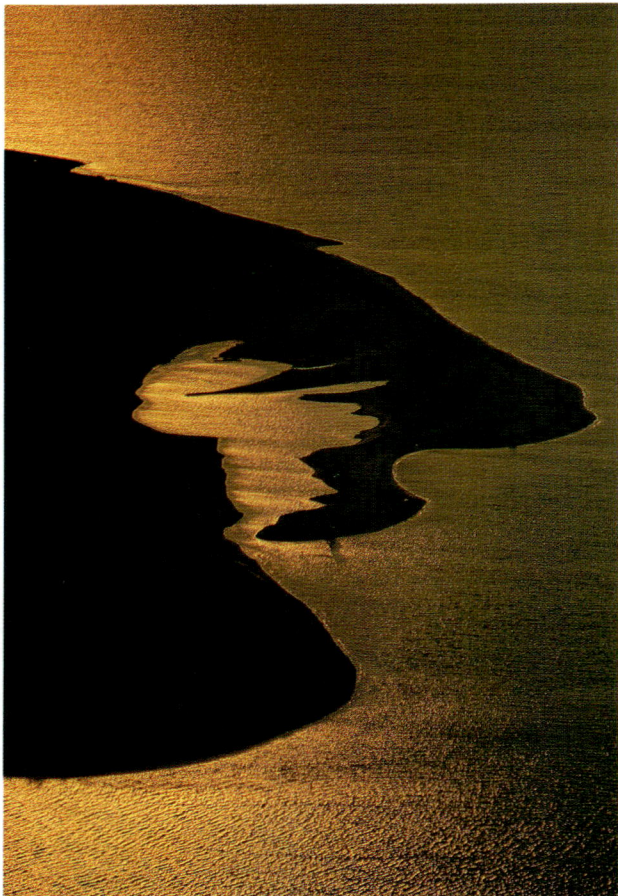

The patterns describing Cape Cod's origins are as visible today as they were 11,000 years ago when the glaciers of the last Ice Age retreated southward, pushing with them the tons of sand and gravel that became the 65-mile-long Cape. The mighty Gulf Stream that washes the coast north of here changes direction off the Cape, leaving in its wake a sea of shoals and shifting sand spits.

Like a beckoning arm, a dark silhouette of Barnstable reaches into the golden surface of the sea *(above)*. Earlier in the day a small skiff explores the shallows off Chatham *(right)*.

*I*t seems a simple thing to find—where the land ends and the sea begins—but not so on Cape Cod. It's all confused by the changing tides, by land appearing and disappearing again, salt water mixing with fresh, the wind shifting the dunes here and there—all complicated by the light that seems to bend and meld ocean to sky.

Beach umbrellas dot the sand on Nantucket Island. The island's name comes from a Wampanoag Indian word meaning "faraway land." Herman Melville described Nantucket as "all beach, without a background," a sentiment no doubt shared by these bathers.

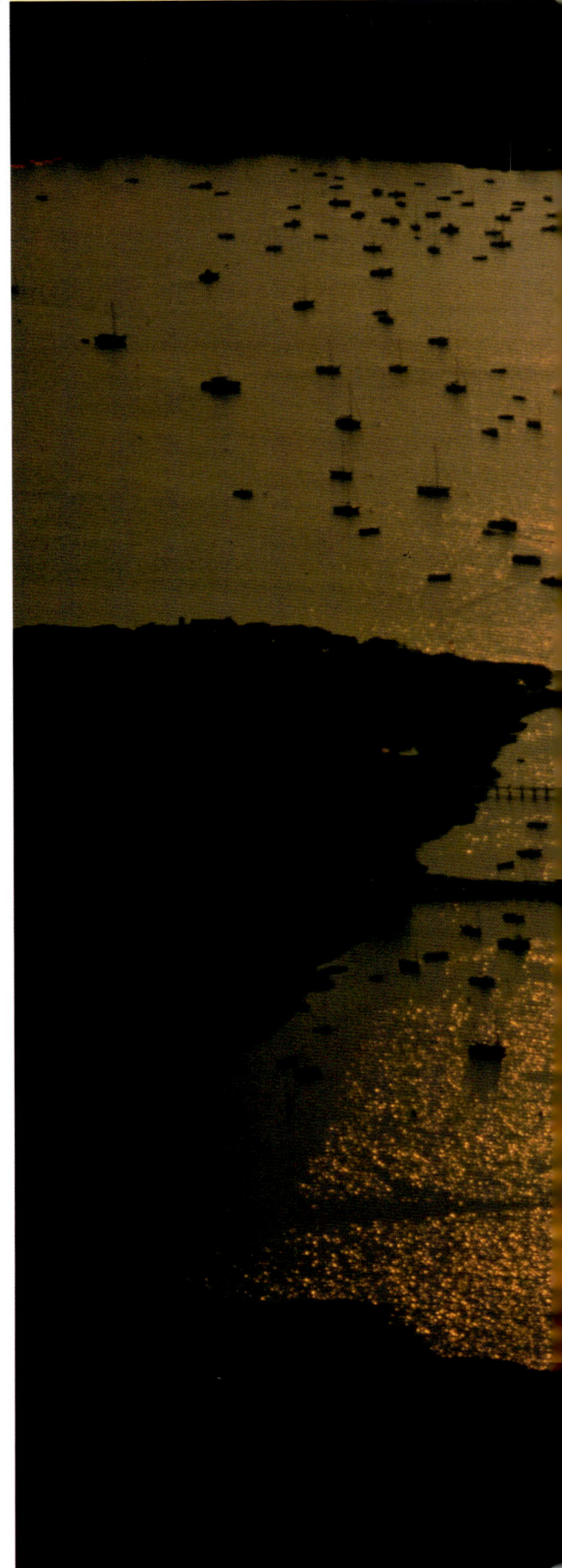

Pleasure yachts mix with a dwindling fleet of fishermen at Chatham Harbor. It was the fish, especially cod, that brought the first Europeans to the coast. Whether the beach-umbrella crowd will replace the old fisherman life on the Cape remains to be seen.

Named for the wild beach plums that grow along its sandy shore, Plum Island stretches off the coast of Newburyport. The southern end of the island is a wildlife refuge where over 250 species of birds have been sighted amidst the dunes and marshes. On the northern tip *(above)* the tiny town of Plum Island is attached to the mainland by a bridge.

In Provincetown (or P-Town, as the locals say) ships, houses and graves all seem to be cut from the same sheet of bright white light. Known in the eighteenth century as "Hell-town" for its wild population of mooncussers and poker sharks, Provincetown has become a gentler haven in the twentieth century. Artists and writers such as Eugene O'Neill, Sinclair Lewis and Jackson Pollock have found inspiration here.

As night approaches, boats return through the gates of Sesuit Harbor. Near Yarmouth at the middle of Cape Cod, this quiet harbor extends for several miles inland.

Green groves of pitch pine stand out along the arid dunes of Sandy Point on the Cape. The pines, planted in 1985 along with beach heather and poverty grass, help hold the fragile ecology intact. Thoreau wrote of the area in his Cape Cod journal: "Barren and desolate country . . . I can find no name for; such a surface perhaps as the sea made into dry land day before yesterday."

North of Boston the coast swings out to Cape Ann, a place as rough as the rocky coast that binds it. Summer houses in Manchester (*above*) are abandoned in the bleak months of winter, but next door in Gloucester (*right*) boats fish for cod and winter flounder throughout the year.

Curving like a wave on a nighttime beach, a long stream of traffic backs up on Route 6 as a summer weekend comes to a close on the Cape.

A necklace of lights encircles the ski slopes at Wachusett Mountain in central Massachusetts. The Mohawk Indians who lived among these wooded hillsides carved a famous footpath across the state's northern tier, known today as the Mohawk Trail.

A country house blends into its snowy environs near Groton. Much is to be discovered about life and weather in New England from such a house. Evergreens, usually Norway spruce, are planted in a row on the north side to block the worst of winter's storms. A maple, with its broad-spreading arms, is planted on the south side. When the heat of summer presses down, the maple's leaves make a cool and shady canopy. In winter, when the sun is welcome, the leaves are gone, and the light comes through. The driveway is a circle; it's easier not to turn around in the snow, or in the mud when spring comes.

The Pilgrims: Roots of a Nation

The Native American Indians preceded them by centuries, perhaps eons. Vikings from Scandinavia discovered New England's shores around the year 1000. The French penetrated a thousand miles into the continent's interior in the early 1500s. Santa Fe had its first governor a quarter century earlier. Virginia's first permanent settlement, at Jamestown, was established in 1607. And when the *Mayflower* set sail from England in 1620, its target was Virginia's James River, not the rocky New England shores to which storms and fate drove it.

Yet to New Englanders and many other Americans, the core of the nation's history somehow dates from those moments in 1620 when the Pilgrims, as their ship lay in anchor in Provincetown Harbor, established a base for future democracy in their remarkable Mayflower Compact.

It was a stern, authoritarian theocracy these dissenters from the Anglican Church established on Massachusetts's shores. Struggles for more religious and civil freedom soon broke out, and within a few years dissenters were striking off to found Rhode Island and other colonies. Yet in Massachusetts, perhaps more than any other colony, a spirit of attachment, community and eventually consent of the governed took root.

Nearly half the Pilgrim settlers died of disease in 1620. But the Pilgrims concluded early treaties with the Indians, and the men plunged into farming, fishing and trading. The women were soon active in

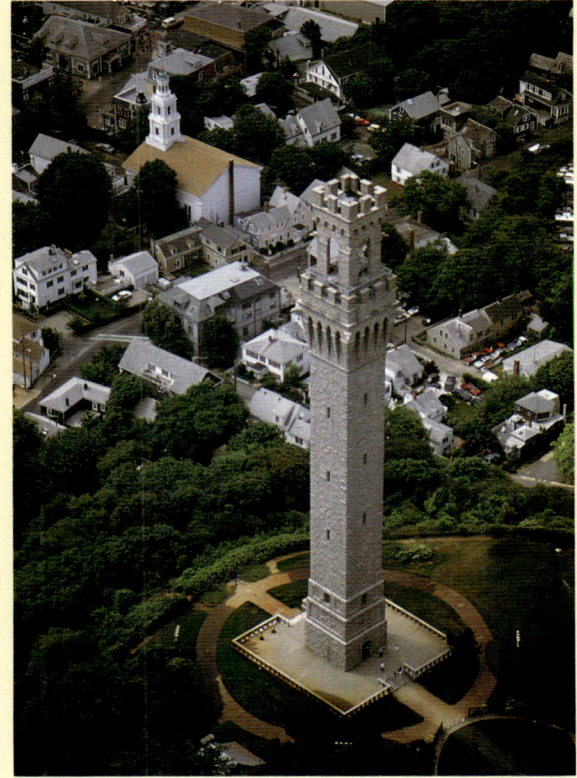

*F*ar left: The *Mayflower II*, a replica of the pilgrim ship, is moored near Plymouth Rock. The clean, orderly grid of the nearby streets might please the strict Puritans, were they to arrive today.

*C*enter: Plimoth Plantation is a contemporary living history museum, a perfect re-creation of the Pilgrim settlement, circa 1627. Miles Standish and William Bradford are here, perfectly dressed down to the buckles on their shoes. The goats and chickens that roam the lanes are the same breeds used by the Pilgrims, specially bred for the plantation.

*A*bove: As the residents of Provincetown never tire of pointing out, the *Mayflower* anchored here before landing at Plymouth. It was here that the Pilgrims drafted the May-flower Compact, signed on November 11, 1620. The Pilgrim Memorial Monument in Province-town commemorates the solemn occasion.

spinning, weaving, candle- and soap-making. Indus-triousness brought its rewards; within a few years the Pilgrims were self-sufficient and prospering.

A 1629 royal act created the Massachusetts Bay Colony. By the century's end, 80,000 English settlers had found their way to these shores, and the Puritans' early theocracy, shattered by numbers and the new society's diversity, passed into history.

Like sentinels of an emerald kingdom,
singular trees punctuate an alfalfa field near
Sturbridge. Dairying and sheepraising have
been the traditional occupations of local
farmers for centuries.

Autumn's golden wash discovers the
hedgerows and roadsides near Brookfield
in central Massachusetts. The "field" at
the end of many place names in the region
dates from when the flat plains were fields
of wild grass and berries. "Greenfield,"
"Springfield" and "Pittsfield" describe the
original features of the land.

The house that Nathaniel Hawthorne immortalized in *The House of the Seven Gables* still stands in Salem. "The aspect of the venerable mansion has always affected me like a human countenance, bearing the traces not merely of outward storm and sunshine, but expressive, also, of the long lapse of mortal life. . . ."

Old Sturbridge Village is a living history re-creation of a farming village in the early 1800s. All of the buildings are New England originals, carefully taken apart, the pieces numbered, then reassembled here.

The industrial boom of the nineteenth century followed the Connecticut River through New England's middle. Logs were floated down the river from New Hampshire to Holyoke (above), where the power of Hadley Falls was harnessed to run this vast mill complex. Miles of canals, built to channel power to various machines, flow through Holyoke, adding charm to the tree-lined paths that now grace the neighborhood.

On April 19, 1775, the "shot heard round the world" was fired at the North Bridge over the Concord River. The American Revolution had begun. Throughout the day fighting continued along this country road, now part of an extensive memorial park.

"*I* am a man of reserved, cold, austere, and forbidding manners," John Quincy Adams once said of himself. The bleak winter facade of the Adams house in Quincy suits the man who owned it well. His parents, John and Abigail Adams, expanded the seven-room clapboard house to a twenty-room mansion, which was home to four generations of the Adams family. In springtime the lawn becomes a lush colonial garden.

Soon after writing a will that included a bequest for a free school, Colonel Ephraim Williams was killed in the French and Indian War of 1755. Williams College in Williamstown was built as he wished. Surrounded by the lush, green Berkshire Hills, the site is among the prettiest in Massachusetts.

In this round barn at Hancock Shaker Village, one man could feed 50 cows at once. Built in 1826, the barn was one of many practical Shaker designs. In 1960 this farm became a museum.

It is small wonder that native poet Emily Dickinson was obsessed with death; the landscape she occupied certainly contained sufficent reminders, like this cemetery in Quincy.

> Because I could not stop for death,
> He kindly stopped for me;
> The carriage held but just ourselves
> And Immortality.

The village of Groton stands in Brueghel-esque splendor beneath a fresh blanket of snow. The limited palette of black, white and gray hides within it a hundred shades. Two private schools, six churches, and a piano in most parlors keep residents busy through the long winter.

*T*he Yale campus in New Haven, Connecticut, is arranged into twelve "colleges," in the English style of Cambridge and Oxford.

*A*bove: More than 24,000 students attend the University of Massachusetts at Amherst. *Above right:* Expensive and exclusive, Bennington College in Vermont is known for its open curriculum and liberal-arts tradition.

A World-Class Center of Learning

Past glory and future hope, New England's universities have been critical to the region's life since 1636, the year Harvard was founded as the New World's first institution of higher learning. With only five percent of America's people, New England today is home to nine percent of the nation's colleges and universities, some 260 in all.

The benefits to New England are economic, intellectual and profound. With students pouring in from across America and across the world, higher education ranks as the major "export" industry of the region. New England easily outstrips national averages in doctorates in every field from physics, mathematics, medicine and chemistry to modern languages and the law. In a typical year some 800,000 full- and part-time students are enrolled. They're big business.

For educational prestige, no region holds a candle to New England. Harvard, Yale, Brown, Dartmouth, MIT and their renowned younger siblings,

from Brandeis and Smith to Amherst, Bowdoin and Williams, are but a fraction of New England's university picture. In terms of student enrollment, Boston's Northeastern University is *the* largest private university in the world.

For New England's world role, the intellectual sparks flowing from academic offices and laboratories are just as critical as student enrollments. New England knowledge built the high-tech era that saved the region's economic skin and gave it a sensational growth platform after World War II. In the 1980s the region was capturing 12 percent of America's academic research and development contracts, and 38 percent of the Department of Defense's research and development contracts to nonprofit institutions.

In the information-based economy of the twenty-first century, intellectual prowess and advance will be more imperative than ever. New England is likely to be ready.

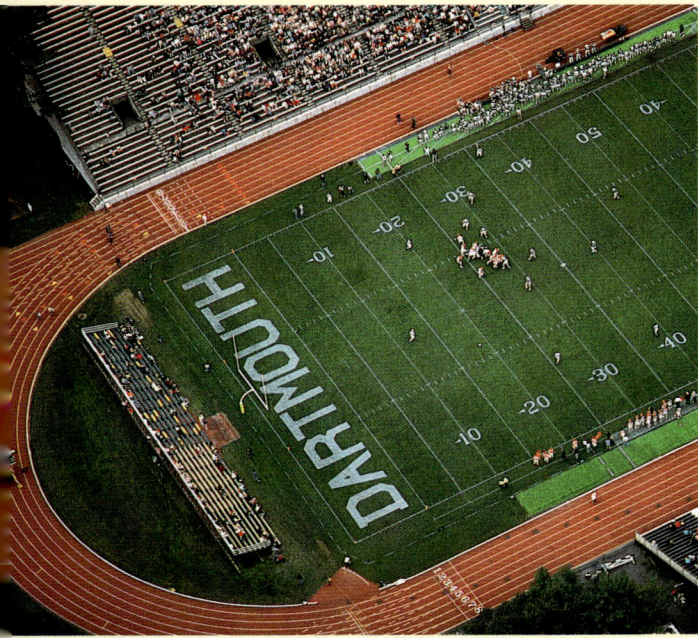

In a gridiron battle of the Ivy Leagues, Dartmouth versus Yale at Dartmouth.

Above: Vermont's Middlebury College, chartered in 1800, features buildings made of local limestone. *Above right:* Wellesley College, in Wellesley, Massachusetts, was America's second women's college, established in 1875.

John F. Kennedy Street passes the triangular Eliot House and the boat house at Harvard.

THE OCEAN STATE

Forestdale
Woonsocket
Wilson Res.
Manville
Pascoag
Rt. 146
Pascoag Res.
Rt. 44
Smithfield
Blackstone R.
Lonsdale
Smith & Sayles Res.
Harmony
Pawtucket
R H O D E   I S L A N D
Rt. 6
Providence
I-195
Scituate Res.
Seekonk R.
I-295
Foster Center
Rt. 102
Clayville
Cranston
Barrington
Coventry
Warwick
Greene
Mt. Hope Bay
Bristol
Flat River Res.
I-95
Rt. 24
West Greenwich
Tiverton
Rt. 1
Narragansett Bay
Prudence Is.
Portsmouth
Nooseneck
Rt. 165
Rt. 102
Conanicut Is.
Rt. 114
Millville
Wickford
Sakonnet R.
Middletown
Hope Valley
Rt. 138
Kingston
Little Compton
Wood R.
I-95
Shannock
Wakefield
Newport
Rt. 1
Rhode Island Sound
Westerly
Point Judith

0   10 miles

Block Is.

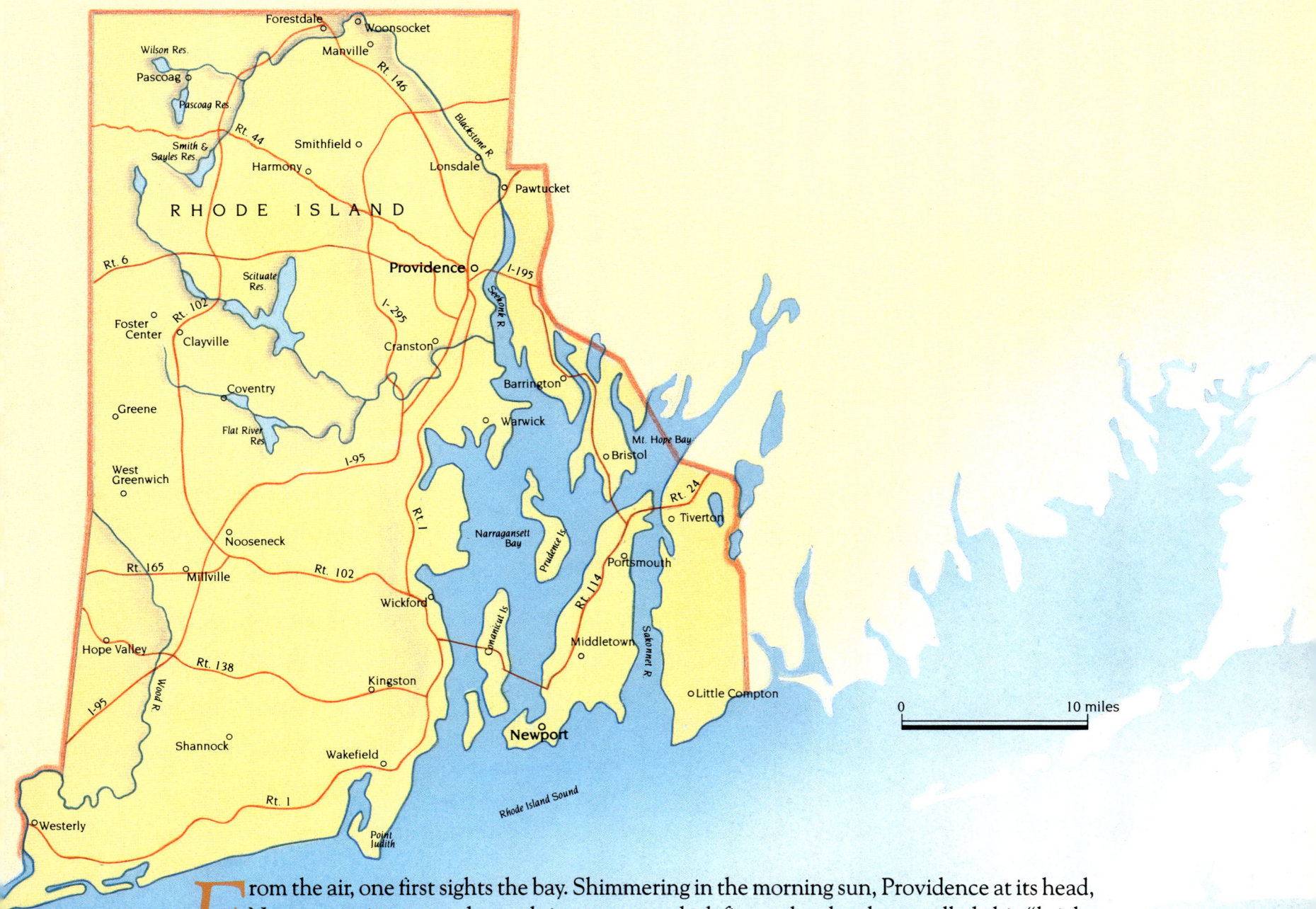

From the air, one first sights the bay. Shimmering in the morning sun, Providence at its head, Newport at its seaward portal, its watery path defines what has been called this "bright sliver of a state." The bay's lovely name, Narragansett, comes from one of the territory's traditional Indian tribes (a proud people subdued, sad to tell, in a bloody battle in 1676). Lining the bay's shores are islands, coves, beaches and some of the Atlantic's great sheltering ports. Physically the bay occupies a quarter of the state's total area. Yet in history and in commerce, in the patterns of people's comings and goings from the days of the Indian tribes onward, Narragansett Bay somehow *is* Rhode Island.

"Little Rhody" has many other distinctive qualities. In a colossal, continent-sized nation, it is positively Lilliputian. It measures but 37 miles east to west, 48 miles north to south. You could fit its 1,214 square miles into Texas 227 times, into Alaska almost 500 times over. Except for the residents of contentedly isolated Block Island, twelve miles off the coast, any resident is within a 45-minute drive of Providence.

Here too is one of America's most closely packed states: some 819 people to the square mile, and lots of industry. Yet Rhode Island is no crowded place of people and houses jammed up to farthest skylines. Instead, outside of the established cities there's an almost spacious feeling—the vastness of the bay, the many natural, unspoiled areas, the woodlands that cover close to a third of the state's surface. In the so-called "South County," the rolling hills, swamps, woodlands and bird sanctuaries remain virtually unscathed by human development.

Left: Newport "cottages" wind along the city's rocky fringe.
Previous pages: A crowded summer ferry pulls into the harbor of Block Island.

Trinity Church, built in 1726, stands in the center of Newport's colonial district. The design of the church was copied by a local craftsman from the Old North Church in Boston; the spires of the two churches are identical. Inside, one can sit where George Washington once sat, and listen to the organ which was tested by Handel before being shipped to the New World.

Since founder Roger Williams fled the oppressive Puritanism of the Massachusetts Bay Colony to settle in Providence in 1636, Rhode Island has honored religious toleration and resistance to tyranny. ("Forced worship stinks in God's nostrils," Williams declared.) Freethinkers, nonconformists and religions of every sort were welcomed. Even when aristocratic elements undermined Williams's "democraticall" government, the urge for freedom burned bright.

Rhode Islanders declared their independence from Great Britain two months before the Declaration of Independence was adopted in Philadelphia in 1776.

In time, a narrow elite of aristocratic families and powerful mercantile interests seized control of Rhode Island's public life. Through means fair and foul, they quashed for decades the aspirations of the vast numbers of Irish, French Canadians, Italians, Poles, Portuguese and others who swelled Rhode Island's population ranks through the nineteenth century and into the twentieth century (making this one of America's most heavily Catholic states). Deep bitterness grew between a Protestant capitalist class and an overwhelmingly Catholic working class. Finally, a mild-mannered Yankee Democratic governor, Theodore Francis Green, led a "bloodless revolution" in 1935 that ended the perennial Republican legislative control and ushered in decades of ethnic-labor-Democratic control. Defending his virtual coup d'état, Green cited Williams's assertion, from three centuries earlier, of the "right of rebellion."

Early Rhode Island capitalized on its fine harbors to prosper in the maritime trade of the 1600s and 1700s. It exported beef, lumber, and fine furniture and jewelry made by early Newport craftsmen, and its skippers pioneered the infamous triangular trade route—to Africa for slaves, to the Caribbean for molasses, finally back to the rum distillers at home. Then, at Pawtucket in the 1790s, Samuel Slater established America's first water-powered cotton mill. Before long, Rhode Island mills were turning out millions of yards of cloth a year and hiring tens of thousands of workers. Textiles prospered until the 1920s, when southern competition broke the industry's back. Ironworking, jewelrymaking and silvermaking flourished, too, making this one of America's most industrialized states.

In the 1970s Rhode Island was in the economic dumps, fearful of its future. The biggest single blow came in 1973 when the state's largest employer, the U.S. Navy, announced it would leave Newport, indeed discontinue almost all operations in the state. Off sailed close to 6,000 jobs and $344 million a year.

Scituate Reservoir is the largest body of fresh water in Rhode Island, lying amidst the dense forests of the state's center. The meandering shorelines are among the best spots to view autumn's color transformations.

Out-migration accelerated. Rhode Island was one of only two American states to lose total population in the decade. So anxious and distrustful were Rhode Islanders that, in the early eighties, they rejected a so-called "Greenhouse Compact" state industrial policy aimed at raising wages and broadening future growth potential by creating industrial innovation through university-based applied research institutes.

But then, in the mid-eighties, New England's high-tech-driven prosperity began to cascade over Rhode Island anyway. So rapid was the boom that fear rose of fast-multiplying tract houses and beaches covered with stilted condos spoiling the primordial openness. Rhode Islanders worried that their state would become one vast, undifferentiated suburb. The legislature, which in times past had rarely been known for environmental innovation, became a vigorous landscape guardian, inaugurating what would soon be hailed as the most expansive effort of open-space purchase—ranked by spending per citizen—amongst all the states.

Providence, Little Rhody's capital and urban center, suffered grave population and economic loss as the industrial era wound down. Like the state as a whole, it suffered periodically from rank political corruption. Yet it had (and has) great treasures. Architecturally, there is College Hill, with its preserved homes of the merchants who got rich off the

127

Above: Divided between old city and new, Providence lies at the head of Narragansett Bay. The marble State House *(foreground)*, built in 1900, boasts the second-largest freestanding dome in the world, surpassed only by St. Peter's in Rome.
Right: Steadfast on a hillside overlooking downtown, Brown University appears untouched by the passing of 226 years.

rum-slave-molasses trade. Academically, the city can claim Brown University, America's seventh oldest. Economically, downtown revival projects started to multiply in the 1980s. And for public buildings, few anywhere outshine the architectural power and simplicity of the State House, its radiant marble walls seeming, in some atmospheric conditions, almost to float over the city.

With its magnificent seascape, mild climate and deepwater harbor, Newport has long been a jewel of the New England coast. Early shipping brought great wealth; then came the sumptuous "cottages" of the 1800s. In more recent times there have been Amer-

ica's Cup races, tennis championships, jazz festivals and the Navy. Modern Newport buffs have worked hard to restore and preserve both the cottages and colonial-era structures in the old town center.

Only by a ferryboat ride of an hour or so will the visitor reach Block Island. Moorlike with its many ponds, a place of towering bluffs of clay, white beaches and colorful old Victorian hotels, the island remains apart from Providence and all of urban New England. Here the small, tightly packed state of Rhode Island kindly offers us an island almost primeval, a place where modernity is an oddity, where time seems to stand still.

*N*ewport's sheltered harbor is one of the great yachting capitals of the world. The Newport-Bermuda Race, the America's Cup and many smaller races attract sailors from far and wide.

*S*cenery from Camelot: the broad green lawns of Hammersmith Farm in Newport witnessed the wedding reception of Jacqueline Bouvier and John F Kennedy in 1953. Newport's oldest working farm, Hammersmith has been in the Auchincloss family since 1887. From 1961 to 1963 the farm served as the Kennedy summer White House; it is now open to the public.

The sleek outline of Block Island floats in the azure waters twelve miles from the mainland. Accessible by ferry, the island is a popular summer retreat, favored for its lovely beaches and lightly developed interior *(above)*. Before the Victorian tourists arrived it was a notorious haunt of pirates and assorted n'er do wells, many of whom made a living scavenging booty from the ships that wrecked off the treacherous south end of "the block." The calmer northern tip of the island *(foreground)* is a national wildlife refuge inhabited only by scavenging seabirds.

Guests gather for a private party at Sakonnet Vineyards on the tip of the Little Compton peninsula. The vines that grow beyond the blue-and-white tents bear grapes that will become well-known Rhode Island vintages such as America's Cup White, Spinnaker White, Eye of the Storm and Compass Rose.

Mullen Hill Road jogs through the verdant countryside near the tiny hamlet of Little Compton. Farmers hereabouts made a major contribution to American gastronomy with the breeding of the Rhode Island red chicken. Separated from the rest of the state by the Sakonnet River, Little Compton preserves the classic rural face of the last century.

Above: When the "cottages" of Newport were built in the 1850s, local fishermen complained of losing their access to the sea. The Cliff Walk, known locally as Fishermen's Walk, was the city's answer. Its narrow white length follows the winding surf past some of America's greatest fortunes and failures. *Right:* The Breakers *(upper left)* dominates its neighbors on Ochre Point.

Walk of Wealth: Newport's Mansions

Palatial "cottages," a strand of American culture as sumptuous and unegalitarian as any in our history, were thrown up in nineteenth-century Newport by the plantation owners, railroad and mining magnates and big-time financiers of a raucous, capitalist nation.

The first was Kingscote, a "Rustick Gothick" mansion reminiscent of English gazebos and garden teahouses, built by the Jones family of Savannah in 1839. The Joneses could claim some gentility, having summered in Newport to escape the South's heats

and fevers for 120 years. But the Northern "royalty" that began ordering one cottage after another following the Civil War were mostly self-made, ostentatious capitalists—the Vanderbilts, Astors, Belmonts, Wideners, Braytons and others.

Cornelius Vanderbilt's Breakers mansion has a dozen varieties of marble, alabaster, silver, massive chandeliers, and a Great Hall with a painted sky 45 feet above the floor. The entire exterior of Mrs. Hermann Oelrichs's Versailles-inspired Rosecliff is of glazed white terra-cotta; inside there is a great heart-shaped stairway. William Wetmore's Château-sur-Mer, renovated in 1872 by architect Richard Morris Hunt, has a three-story hall and a dining room of

elaborately carved walnut decorated with leather. Mrs. Stuyvesant Fish had to have two ballrooms in her house.

Conceived by wealthy Southerners before the Civil War and carried to its zenith by Northern capitalists in the Gilded Age afterward, the culture of the Newport mansions came crashing down with the introduction of the federal income tax and then the great stock market crash of 1929. Today the social pretensions, and wealth, are long since washed away. But the houses remain, some now owned by preservation groups. For spectacular walks, few in America equal the pathway that skirts the great cottage lawns on one side, the deep blue Atlantic on the other.

*F*ort Adams stands guard at the entrance to Narragansett Bay. Built of granite hauled from quarries in Maine, the fort served as a strategic defense post for all of southern New England. Though never engaged in military action, Fort Adams guarded the Navy's entire Atlantic Fleet in the early 1900s and was occupied until 1945.

A yellow Stearman biplane soars over the compact farmland near Tiverton, one of the few areas in Rhode Island where farming is still the mainstay. Lying just a few miles from Massachusetts, Tiverton was part of Plymouth Colony until 1692.

*A*cross the waters of Narragansett Bay, a promising sunrise climbs above an ocean of treetops, coaxing the hidden houses of West Greenwich out of the morning fog.

THE SOUND
AND THE RIVER

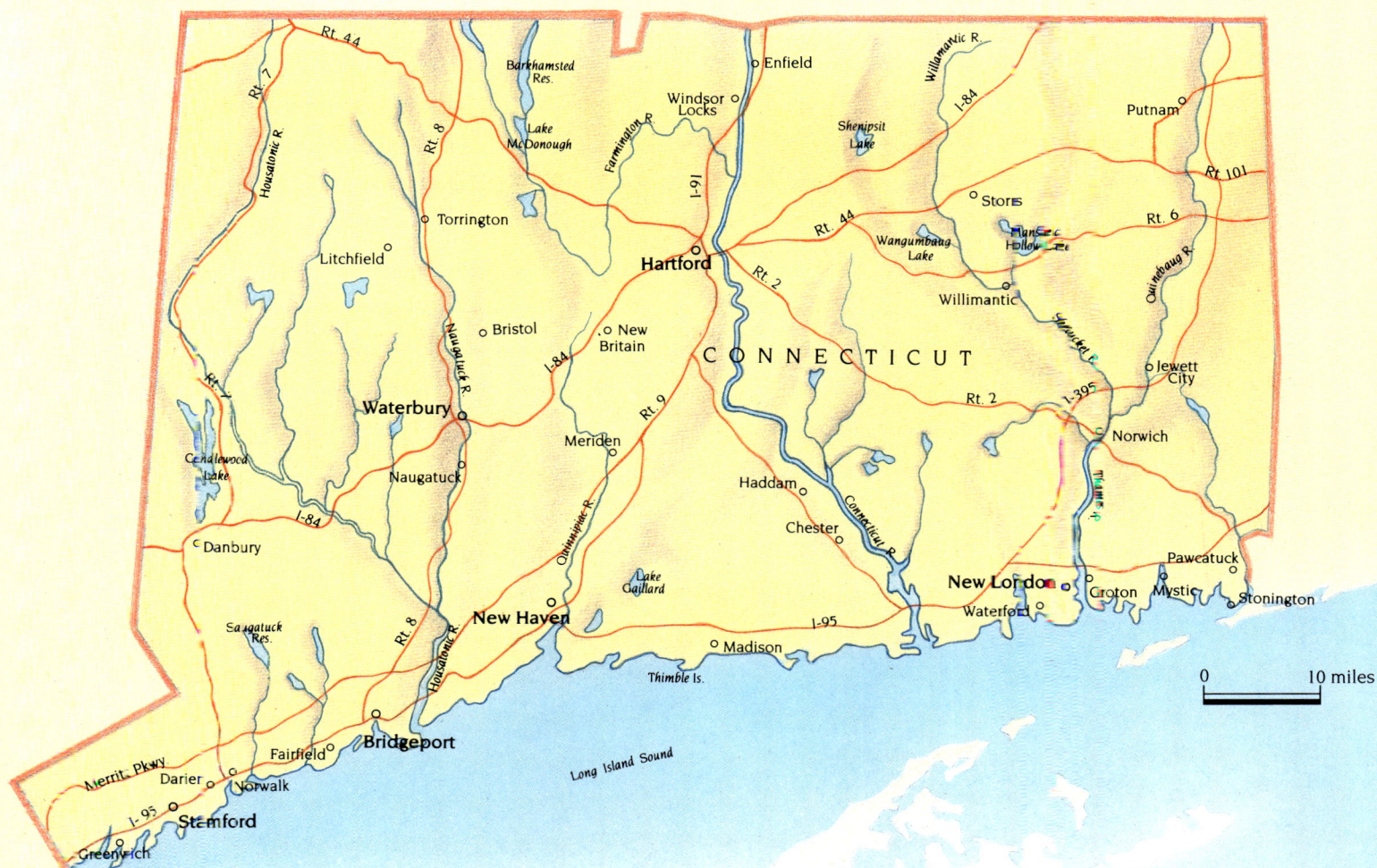

Map of Connecticut showing cities, rivers, and roads

Half sizzling modern metroplex, half serene old New England, late twentieth-century Connecticut sways between two geographies, two world views, alternative futures.

Here is a compact civilization: 5,018 square miles (third smallest among American states) but 3,366,300 souls, which qualifies for the country's fourth-highest population density. In certain regions of this "worthy little state," as John Gunther once called it, one can find the people packed in closely together, 88 percent of the state population in twelve metropolitan areas.

The heart of ultra-urban Connecticut lies in the industrial belt which runs from Hartford, the state capital and rough state geographic center, south past New Britain and Waterbury toward New Haven. From there the densely packed belt veers southwesterly along Long Island Sound through Bridgeport, Fairfield, Norwalk and Stamford to encompass affluent, increasingly urbanized Fairfield County—territory with closer economic and emotional ties to New York City than to Hartford.

But there is also a more placid, less densely packed Connecticut. The Atlantic coastline, rockbound and rugged with sandy beaches and salt meadows backed by a mildly rolling upland, is typically New England. Along its shores are such port cities as New London, Groton and Mystic, an old whaling port which boasts a magnificent maritime museum. To the west rise the Berkshire Hills, the private-school center of America, with some of the wildest and most spectacular scenery in eastern America. Perfectly preserved New England villages, with their central greens and beautiful colonial homes, grace western and central Connecticut. One of the most exquisite is old Litchfield, birthplace of Harriet Beecher Stowe, where the town center has been declared a historical district.

Left: The village of Litchfield shows the dignified face of classic Connecticut.
Previous pages: The Housatonic River meanders along the foot of the Berkshire Hills in the state's quiet northwest corner.

*H*artford, the state capital and America's insurance capital, rises from the banks of the Connecticut River. Behind its businesslike appearance Hartford shelters diverse ethnic neighborhoods, with Puerto Ricans, Jamaicans, blacks and Irish mixing with Connecticut Yankees.

Increasingly urbanized, the Connecticut River Valley still offers farmland scenes reminiscent of what Thomas Pownall, writing in 1796, described as "a rich, well cultivated vale thickly settled and swarming with people." To the east, in towns that decades ago lost their textile base, there is surprising lightness of population; airplane pilots find here one of the few dark nighttime spots on the urbanized eastern seaboard corridor from Boston to Washington, D.C.

Connecticut has been judged proud, wealthy, politically clean, independent of mind, mechanically inventive. In its early years, it was to a man and woman Yankee Congregationalist. In time, however, many of the Yankees departed the flinty soil of their

birth to seek their fortunes on more fertile soils westward. The first great "ethnic" population wave came with the Irish immigrants fleeing the potato famine of 1846–47. They were followed by Germans, Scandinavians, Italians and Poles in such numbers that Connecticut in 1920 trailed only Massachusetts and Rhode Island in percentages of foreign-born residents. Now Connecticut is seven percent black, four percent Hispanic—figures likely to double by the year 2000.

Why is Connecticut called the Constitution State? Because the Fundamental Orders, drafted in 1639 from a sermon by the colony's founder, Thomas Hooker, represented the first constitution drafted in the New World. Hooker came to escape Massachusetts's autocratic and theocratic government, but no radical was he. Town-based independence and Congregational order, Puritan temperament, life on harsh soil—all fed into this state's quite special character. Connecticut was an early leader in public and private education. It fostered inventors, and in time great wealth.

Shrewd Yankee peddlers, tinkerers, inventors, machine and then factory shop owners—all appeared early on the Connecticut scene and left an indelible mark. Colonel Samuel Colt pioneered advanced pistols, Eli Whitney the cotton gin, and both "invented" the idea of interchangeable parts, critical to the Industrial Revolution. Charles Goodyear, also a Connecticut man, developed the vulcanizing process for rubber. New Haven alone claims invention of the pizza, the hamburger, the lollipop, the frisbee, the game of football, the submarine, the erector set, the telephone switchboard and the corkscrew.

Connecticut's metropolitan areas have not seen quite the explosiveness of suburban growth that depleted so many older American cities of their downtowns, retail cores and job bases. Hartford is much poorer than the more privileged suburbs that surround it; statistics show it to be America's fourth-poorest city. But the great insurance firms have not deserted Hartford and have in fact provided enlightened leadership in urban renewal and outreach to the poor and minorities. Hartford has such treasures as its Old State House, a lovely colonial masterpiece designed by Charles Bulfinch in 1796, and the Beaux Arts-style buildings surrounding the Gothic-style state capitol in Bushnell Park. But massive highrises have been erected, and the city let superhighways cut itself off from the beautiful, expansive Connecticut River. One downtown interstate interchange is a wild mess of crossovers and crazy exits, among the nation's worst. Hartford has magnificent parks but also Airport Road, a generic strip of fast-food joints, poles, wires, neon and clutter that's the literal antithesis of neat, ordered, graceful old Connecticut.

New Haven, home of Yale, Connecticut's great university, was a 1950s and 1960s leader in urban renewal—some of the results positive, others not. By the 1980s the wrecking ball had given way to historic preservation, endemic "town-gown" hostilities had cooled down, and Yale was an active, investing partner in broad-scale downtown and neighborhood

*I*n Fairfield the opulent homes of well-to-do professionals open onto Long Island Sound.

The generation who grew up in Stamford in the 1950s and 1960s barely recognize the place today. What was then a faded old industrial town attuned to commuter trains to New York City (42 miles away) has become a corporate center of highrise offices and convention centers. Some critics refer to the new, coolly impersonal Stamford as "the Houston of New England."

revival. New Haven also fought long, hard and successfully to stop suburban malls that might have blown away its retail base.

Industrial Bridgeport, Connecticut's largest city, a lusty Industrial Revolution town and hometown of the great showman P.T. Barnum, declined so precipitously in the mid-twentieth century that Paul Newman called it "the armpit of New England." Graft and tolerance for crime, in a state proud of its clean politics, thrived too. But in the eighties, strong economic development and neighborhood revival efforts were launched, with major business backing.

Then there's Stamford: the sleepy, decaying little industrial city of the 1950s that switched from blue to white collar with a vengeance, as wave upon wave of corporations moved the 42 miles from Manhattan. Xerox, GTE, Champion International, Singer, Pitney Bowes and other companies came to town, most throwing up gleaming, cold, impersonal office build-

Merritt Parkway, the highway builders' best of the 1930s, evidences a gracious landscaping rarely repeated in the age of the interstates.

ings with their terraces and greenery tucked away from the sidewalk, inaccessible to the public. Lots of jobs and new wealth came in the wake, but also an icy bleakness at the downtown street level—some call it the city's "Houstonization," or "Stamford Sterile." Stamford also accentuates the problem of all of prosperous Fairfield County: a vast excess of jobs over affordable housing.

Connecticut almost always shows up as the top per capita income state in the country. Poverty rates are low, property values high. Education rates, teacher salaries, citizens listed in Who's Who—all are high. But Connecticut rarely contributes major leaders to national life. And its state government is competent but unexciting. The old nickname "State of Steady Habits" still fits.

Three-story rowhouses, like these in Hartford, are a feature of working-class neighborhoods all over New England.

Laid out in nine equal squares by the Puritans in 1638, the New Haven Green makes a fine place to gather for the summer-long jazz festival and a bit of sunbathing. The Puritans might find the gathering somewhat wild, but Henry Ward Beecher, who preached against slavery from the steps of the United Congregational Church *(upper left)* in 1855, would probably advocate the freedom of all to choose.

*B*ehind New Haven's utilitarian
waterfront lie a newly vibrant downtown,
the grounds of Yale University and
poor neighborhoods strongly revitalized
in the 1980s.

ALEX S. MACLEAN/LANDSLIDES

Above: Shade-grown tobacco is still cultivated in the Tobacco Valley, along the Connecticut River north of Hartford. The gray-brown color of the fields comes from nets that are put over the plants for shade. The ripe crop is hung to dry in the long, narrow tobacco barns. Connecticut's tobacco is used mainly for cigar wrappers.

Right: Near Madison on Long Island Sound, the artful meander of water through a coastal marsh is quickly being replaced by the less graceful, more rigid paths of driveways in a housing development. Environmentalists bemoan the decline of the coastal wetlands, as more and more waterfront is reshaped according to the "needs" of man.

There is nothing mysterious in the clean, classic lines of the village of Mystic *(above)*. Some of the fastest clipper ships on the Atlantic were built here in the nineteenth century. Today Mystic is better known for its excellent Seaport Museum, though to the fleet of Portuguese fishermen who work the waters here, a living from the sea is still a daily reality.

Pleasure Beach on Long Island Sound *(right)* appears to be just that.

The Thimble Islands off the coast of New Haven *(opposite)* make up a Lilliputian land of summer cottages, diminutive boat piers and thumb-sized beaches. The "islets" are no small affair to visitors, however, who arrive in giant hordes.

A woman and her Irish setter have just
arrived via a red sportscar at their summer
home near Litchfield. Ages away from the
working farm that once occupied these
dark barns, this property has crossed the
boundary from utility to luxury. Barns
converted to studios, and cornfields given
over to immense lawns of mown grass,
characterize the changing countryside.
The restoration of such places alongside
the traditional life of the farmers nearby
is one of the ongoing ironies of the New
England countryside.

Warm days and cold nights produce the best display of color in the autumn woods of Connecticut. Country inns and hotels are booked months in advance for late September and October, when thousands of "leafers" flock to the countryside to witness the pyrotechnics. The pigments that "appear" on the leaves have always been present and are simply made visible by the breakdown of the dominant green chlorophyll.

Visible through a lattice of winter trees,
old stone fences surround a lonely woodland
cottage near Norwich.

This farm near Litchfield (*right*) is a modern
dairy operation, as busy in winter as summer.
Though today Connecticut is primarily a
manufacturing state, resident farmers man-
age to produce enough milk, eggs, chicken
and vegetables to keep the locals fed.

A timeless image of labor and reward,
an old factory stands frozen on the banks
of the Quinebaug River in Jewett City.
Though labor was plentiful, rewards were
small. The eight-hour workday, signed into
law in 1867, was widely ignored; fourteen
hours was the normal shift, for which
unskilled workers earned $1 per day,
skilled workers $3.50.

A silver-lined fog lifts off the tiny
Connecticut River town of Chester
in Middlesex County.

The star-shaped ruins of Fort Griswold on the Thames River at Groton mark an act of bloody treachery unequaled in the annals of the Revolution. In 1781, 140 American patriots under William Ledyard met here with 800 British soldiers. The patriots fought valiantly to defend the fort but, realizing they were greatly outnumbered, surrendered. When Ledyard handed his sword to a Tory officer, the officer used it to stab him through. Many of the American soldiers, who had already cast their arms aside, were then shot or bayoneted to death, and many of the bodies mutilated. Today a state park and a 135-foot monument commemorate the victims of the Griswold Massacre.

The Harkness Estate at Waterford was given to the people of the Constitution State by philanthropist Edward S. Harkness and his wife, Mary. "Eolia," as they called their Italianate home, is surrounded by 234 acres of elegant parterre gardens and broad lawns that reach to the edge of Long Island Sound.

Joined at its base to Darien, the exclusive point known as Long Neck glides onto Long Island Sound (above). It is an area favored by prosperous professionals who work in Manhattan, 50 miles to the south.

Everything points to the sea in Stonington (right), a thriving fishing village settled in 1735. Like any seagoing town, it is a place with stories to tell. There are the wolf-stones—large slabs placed over local graves to keep the once numerous wolves from digging up the bones of the dead. Then there's the local boy Nat Palmer, who discovered part of Antarctica; the great clipper ships that once sailed from the tip of Water Street; and the War of 1812 battle in which residents defended the town against five British warships with just two small cannons—and won.

A nuclear submarine stops for servicing at the U.S. Naval Submarine Base in Groton. Many submarines are built at the nearby General Dynamics shipyard, where the USS *Nautilus*, the first atomic-powered submarine, was constructed in 1954. More than 14,000 military personnel, including the crews of 30 subs, are a vital part of the area's economy.

New London's links with the outside world converge at the Thames River waterfront: the Union Railroad station, a ferryboat bound for Long Island, and the old main highway to Boston. If this waterfront lacks the colonial charm of other Connecticut ports, part of the blame goes to Benedict Arnold, the locally born "turncoat" who burned most of the city during the Revolution.

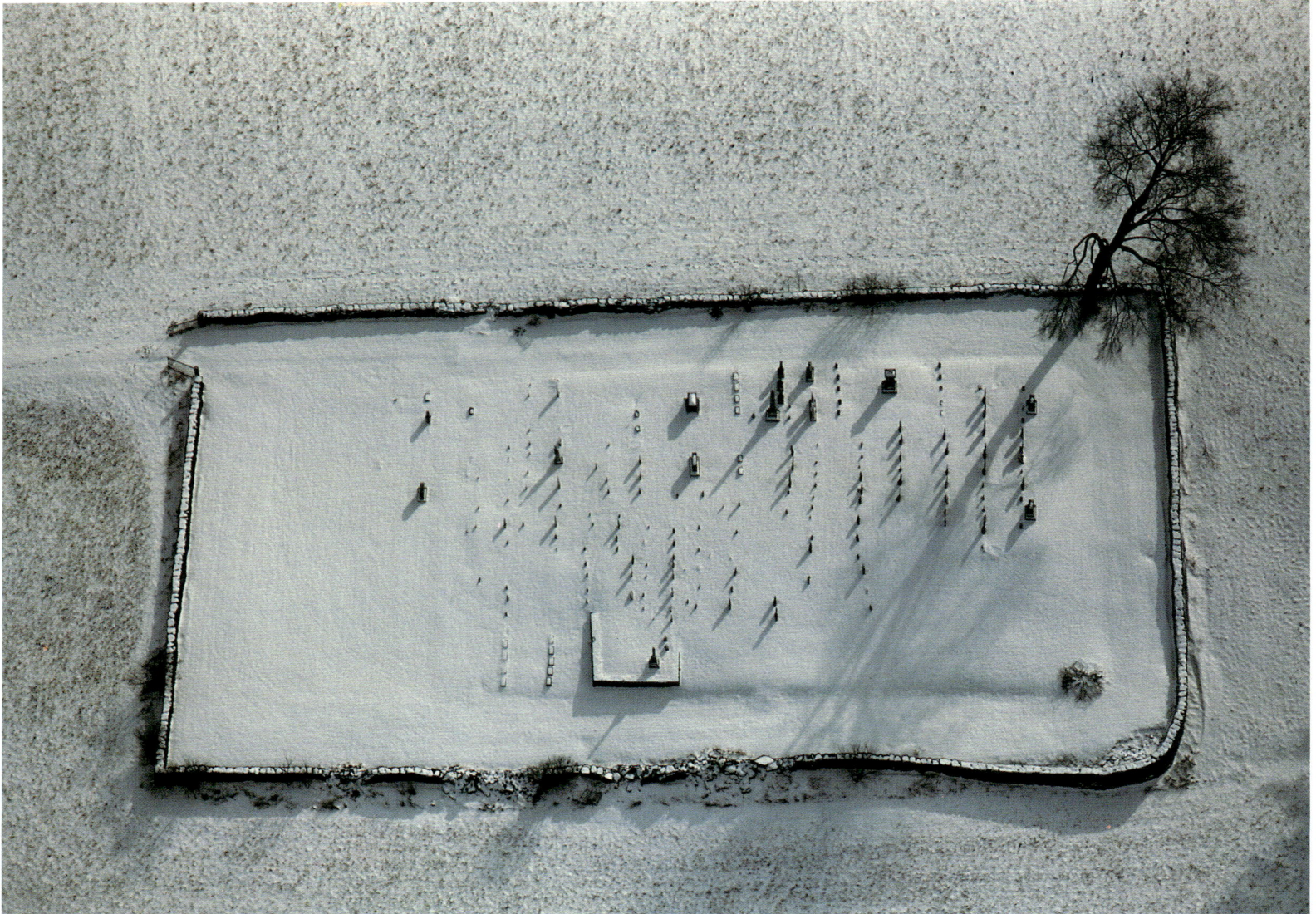

Stone fences protect the memory of the dead from
the undifferentiated whiteness of a New England winter.
The poet Wallace Stevens (who was also an insurance
executive in Hartford) was familiar with landscapes like
these when he wrote:

> It was evening all afternoon.
> It was snowing
> And it was going to snow.
> The blackbird sat
> In the cedar-limbs.

("Thirteen Ways of Looking at a Blackbird")

In a snowy scene near Packer,
a stream catches the morning light.

GENTLE FIELD AND HILL

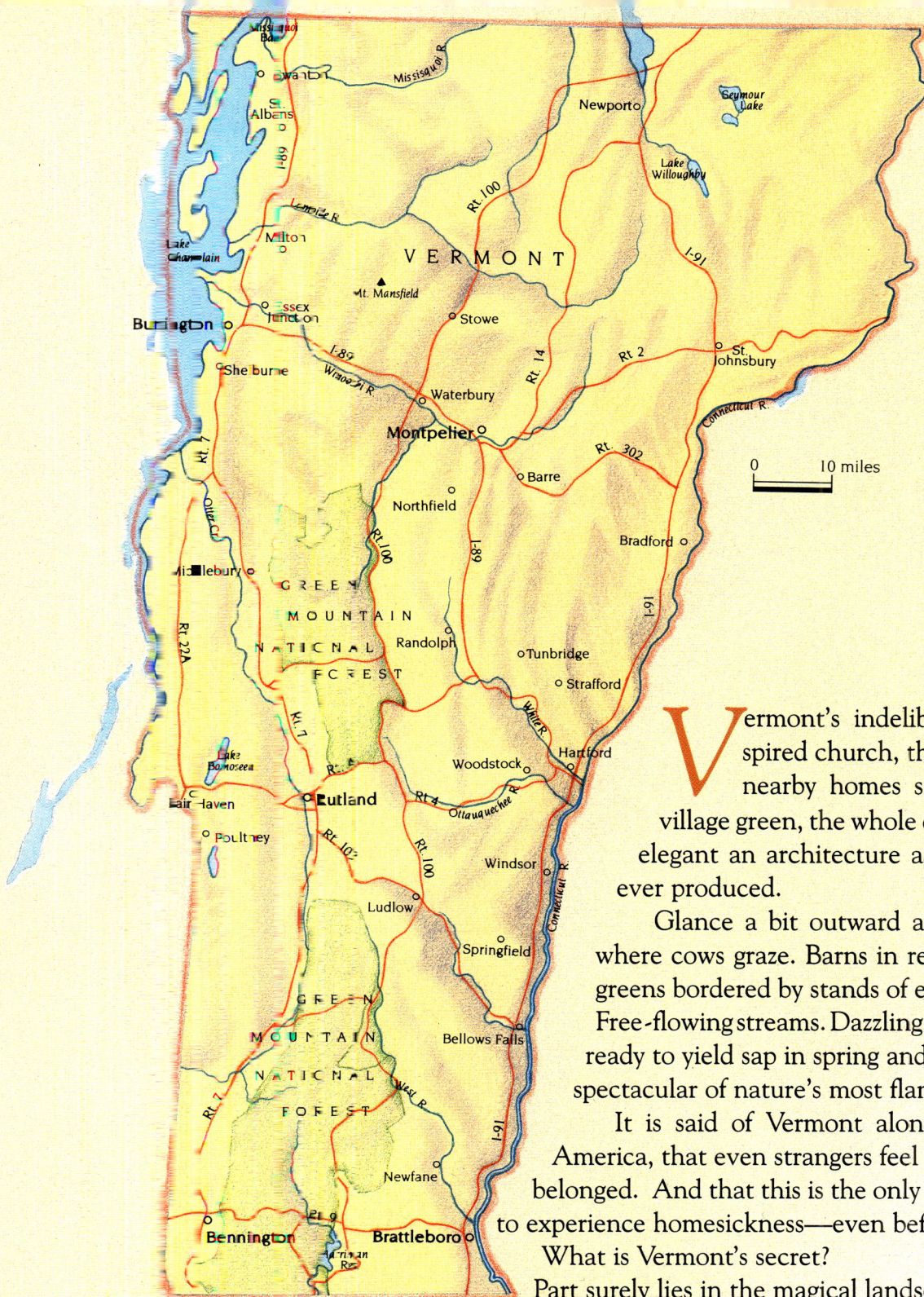

Vermont map with labels:

Swanton, St. Albans, Milton, Lake Champlain, Burlington, Essex Junction, Shelburne, Missisquoi R., Newport, Seymour Lake, Lake Willoughby, VERMONT, Mt. Mansfield, Stowe, Lamoille R., Rt. 100, I-91, St. Johnsbury, Winooski R., Waterbury, Rt. 14, Rt. 2, Montpelier, Barre, Rt. 302, Connecticut R., Northfield, Bradford, GREEN MOUNTAIN NATIONAL FOREST, Randolph, Tunbridge, Strafford, Middlebury, Rt. 22A, White R., Hartford, Woodstock, Lake Bomoseen, Rutland, Ottauquechee R., Rt. 4, Fair Haven, Poultney, Rt. 103, Rt. 100, Windsor, Ludlow, Springfield, GREEN MOUNTAIN NATIONAL FOREST, Bellows Falls, Rt. 7, Newfane, West R., I-91, Rt. 9, Bennington, Brattleboro, Harriman Res.

0   10 miles

V ermont's indelible image is of the white-spired church, the sturdy meetinghouse and nearby homes surrounding a commodious village green, the whole constructed in as simple and elegant an architecture as American civilization has ever produced.

Glance a bit outward and you see gentle pastures where cows graze. Barns in red or white. Forests of evergreens bordered by stands of erect, graceful white birches. Free-flowing streams. Dazzling arrays of wildflowers. Maples ready to yield sap in spring and then produce an autumnal spectacular of nature's most flaming red.

It is said of Vermont alone, among the 50 states of America, that even strangers feel instantly at home, as if they belonged. And that this is the only state for which people seem to experience homesickness—even before they've left.

What is Vermont's secret?

Part surely lies in the magical landscape of gentle field and hill. Like New Hampshire's Whites, Vermont has its Green Mountains. The difference is that the Greens, geologically much older, are less craggy, softer, more climbable, more comprehensible. The setting they create makes man seem instantly welcome.

So exquisite and prized is the state's environment of hill, valley, pasture and river that Vermonters go to special lengths to defend it. They led America in banning commercial billboards along their highways. In the early seventies they passed their epochal Act 250, which turned back ill-advised real estate developments, whether they be massive ski-condo villages or shopping centers, and forced ones that were approved to be more environmentally benign. The Vermont legislature trailed only Oregon's in banning nonreturnable bottles and cans. By the late eighties the state government was requiring towns to create careful physical development plans and submit them for state review. Localities were granted substantial latitude, but the legislature made it clear that it wanted to protect the irreplaceable Vermont environment by discouraging strip

Left: Route 9 leads to the First Congregational Church in Old Bennington, a town landmark since 1806. The grave of poet Robert Frost can be found among those in the shady churchyard. *Previous pages:* The village of Woodstock spreads through the lush foothills of the Green Mountains.

Above: Route 125 cuts through Middlebury Gap in the Green Mountains. Though it is only September, the cold comes quickly to the mountains here above 3,000 feet. *Right:* The rising light of morning skims across the rooftops of a Burlington neighborhood.

highway development and encouraging compact, lively city and town centers.

The Vermont secret relates intimately to character, too. Historically isolated, the state was bound to change with the advent of mass communications—and especially as thousands of urban refugees, attracted perhaps by Vermont's primal innocence but bringing all their differing lifestyles in tow, came packing in from New York, Massachusetts, Connecticut and other points south from the 1960s onward.

Still, Vermont has remained largely itself. Echoes of its legendary character resonate, like Puritanism, into today: hardiness, simplicity, thriftiness, self-reliance. The state's political folk hero of the twentieth century, the late U.S. senator George Aiken, embodied it all: a simple farmer, nobody's fool in matters

intellectual, innovative governor in the thirties, battler for public power against private interests. In 1966 Aiken produced the brilliant Vietnam peace plan that could have saved not only Lyndon Johnson's place in history but thousands of Vietnamese and American lives: "The U.S. should declare victory and get out."

Vermonters even tolerate a measure of radicalism: in the 1980s, for example, Burlington citizens elected one of the few socialist mayors ever in the United States. In 1982 Vermont town meetings grabbed national attention by voting for a freeze on nuclear weapons. Indeed, the state's very origins were a touch radical: pressed by competing pre-Revolutionary land claims by both New York and New Hampshire, Vermonters hired Ethan Allen, a brash 27-year-old, as colonel-commandant of a military company to defend their interests. Allen's Green Mountain Boys did well in skirmishes with New York, then scored a stunning Revolutionary War victory by helping to defeat General Burgoyne's troops at the Battle of Bennington in 1777. For thirteen years, until New York's claims receded, Vermont functioned as a sovereign republic with its own currency, postal service and foreign relations. The constitution of the Republic of Vermont broke historic ground in America by totally prohibiting slavery and declaring universal manhood suffrage, without the requirement of owning property.

Vermont finally joined the American Union, as the fourteenth state, in 1791. But it remained a toughly principled society. It opposed the national Federalists as too closely allied to the propertied and rich. It championed abolitionism, to end slavery forever in America, with rare fervor. Vermont was literally Republican before Lincoln became president (voting 4-to-1 for John Fremont, the first Republican presidential candidate, in 1856, and remaining steadfastly Republican for a century afterward). During the Civil War, half of Vermont's men of military age joined the Union army. One of every seven lost his life. The war's toll was so deep, the state so exhausted, that Vermont slipped into the economic doldrums and a kind of political malaise that would not lift until after World War II.

*T*he heavens open between colliding clouds over the Connecticut River *(above)*. According to a local saying, "Evening red and morning gray sends the traveler on his way."

Industry figured in Vermont's history: quarries for the famous Vermont marble, paper mills, woolen mills, machine tools. But the state was distant from main rail lines and remained overwhelmingly rural. In the nineteenth century Vermont was a great sheep state; in the twentieth it became America's most intensive dairy state. Rapid population and economic gains came in the sixties with such historic events as the arrival of IBM (which set up a major plant at Burlington), a literal explosion in the ski and summer resort business, and hordes of new summer residents and retirees. The interstates, say some, have made Vermont a virtual suburb of Massachusetts and New York. Prolonged, bitter fights have swirled around big tourist developments and the traffic and unsightly strip development they seem to bring in their wake.

To the east, the Connecticut River and its lovely valley quite neatly separate Vermont from New Hampshire. In the west, lovely Lake Champlain, down which Samuel de Champlain sailed to gain the

Granite is extracted from the largest quarries in the country at Barre, "Granite Center of the World" (*above*). The quarries here, all owned by the Rock of Ages Company, supply America with nearly one-third of its gravestones.

white man's first view of Vermont in 1609, provides 112 miles of border. Thriving and multifaceted Burlington, biggest town in a state of very small cities, enjoys a spirit-lifting view of the lake.

The territory east and west of the Green Mountains used to be Vermont's critical division. Today the division is more north-south. Prospering southern Vermont is close to the East Coast megalopolis and is increasingly impacted by ski and tourist areas. Northern Vermont by contrast, offers little affluence

outside the Burlington and Barre-Montpelier areas. Here, in the so-called Northeast Kingdom along the Canadian and New Hampshire borders, one finds Vermont's most serious isolation and poverty.

It's easy to imagine the metropolitan development push one day touching, and changing, every corner of this intimate little state. That such growth brings wealth, few question. But should it be welcomed? Vermont, so desperately anxious to remain its own special, set-apart place, is not sure.

The curious grounds of the Shelburne Museum (*left*) somewhat resemble a large-scale folk-art painting, and indeed the folk art collection here is among the finest in the world. The museum is home to 35 buildings of various architectural styles, brought from around the region. The last steamship to work nearby Lake Champlain, the *Ticonderoga,* made its way here overland and is even supplied with a lighthouse.

The round barn on this dairy farm near Bradford (*right*) escaped the collectors from the Shelburne Museum and is joined now by a modern milk storage tank. Much of Vermont's "white gold" supplies the urban populations of Boston and New York.

Long winter shadows accompany the figures of skiers gliding to the end of a run after a day of skiing in the Green Mountains. Skiing was popular in Vermont as early as the 1920s, and in 1934 America's first ski lift was built in Woodstock. Unlike the gondola here, the first lift was a rope tow powered by a Model-T engine.

Following pages: A temporary village of ice-fishing shanties dots the frozen surface of Lake Champlain. The typical shanty is an eight-foot-long structure (the right size for a pickup truck) and is equipped with a heater, a bench and a very deep hole in the floor. Land-locked salmon, stranded in the lake since the last Ice Age, are among the many fish that bite.

*I*t has been said that a Vermont year is "nine months of winter and three months of damn poor sleddin'." This parent-child bobsled team *(left)* is taking advantage of the short season.

*S*kiing, skating, sledding, sleighing and snowmobiling keep Vermont's population mobile through the deep freeze. Ice sailing *(right)*, a winter version of windsurfing, is gaining popularity on Lake Champlain near Burlington. Drifting snow even supplies the simulation of breaking surf.

Ski trails crisscross four of Killington's six mountains *(left)*. The first ski trails in Vermont were cleared by the Civilian Conservation Corps during the Great Depression. Now there are more than 878 trails statewide, generating a $300-million annual business.

Morgan horses frolic on the green meadows at the UVM Morgan Horse Farm in Middlebury (*left*). The sturdy Morgan (favored by police in city parks) originated in Vermont in the 1780s with a man named Justin Morgan and a stallion of the same name.

Strafford, population 731, lies along the Ompompanoosuc River in Orange County (*right*). The former church is now the meetingplace for Strafford township, or "town" as they say in Vermont. There are 246 such "organized" towns in Vermont, and at last count several "unorganized" ones. In rural enclaves like these, that remnant of pure democracy known as the town meeting thrives.

The village of Newfane in southern Vermont is a classic of early nineteenth-century design. Presiding over the town green *(center)*, the Windham County Courthouse (1825) displays the dignified countenance of its Greek Revival design. In matching style the First Congregational Church (1839) stands on its flank. The nearby Union Hall (1832) displays the Gothic flourishes that would soon be all the rage. Pristine white houses, all protected by the National Register, brighten nearby streets. The uniform scale, spacing and graceful landscaping of Newfane make it a New England village for the true connoisseur.

The "Tunbridge World's Fair" has been
a major attraction in tiny Tunbridge since
1851. More than 20,000 people have been
known to descend on the hamlet of 900 for
the fair each September. They come to
watch the ox pull, see the giant cheeses and
to make merry at the state's most infamous
rural revel. In the old days anyone at the fair
who was still sober by three P.M. was
rounded up and asked to go home.

The Waterbury Reservoir, surrounded by parklands and forests, stretches through a sheltered valley in the Green Mountains. In the distance, Mount Mansfield and the adjoining hills "are alive with the sound of music." The descendants of the Von Trapp family, immortalized in the film *The Sound of Music,* run a ski lodge there.

The era of water transport flows nicely
into the electronic age in Bellows Falls. The
hydroelectric power station here has been
operating on the Connecticut River
since 1928. The canal that channels water
to the plant was originally built in 1802 as a
bypass for ships around the falls.

*B*urlington, Vermont's largest city, has
the good fortune of being situated on
a hillside between the Green Mountains
and Lake Champlain.

*T*he 306-foot spire of the Bennington
Battle Monument commemorates a fight
that actually took place in New York, four
miles away. There on August 16, 1777,
the Green Mountain Boys defeated British
troops who were trying to capture supplies
from the depot in Bennington (which stood
where the monument is now). The resulting
British supply shortage was a crucial
turning point in the Revolution.

GENTLE FIELD AND HILL

The steely blue waters of Missisquoi Bay separate northern Vermont from Canada (*left*). The skyline of Montreal, 55 miles to the northwest, is just visible on the foggy horizon. French Canadians, or *Quebecois*, have constituted a large ethnic minority in the northern counties since the nineteenth century, when they settled much of the farmland.

The Missisquoi River (*right*) carries the waters of the Green Mountains through the broad plains of the Champlain Valley to Lake Champlain. *Missisquoi* is an Abenaki word interpreted variously as "great grassy meadows," "big woman" or "place of much slate."

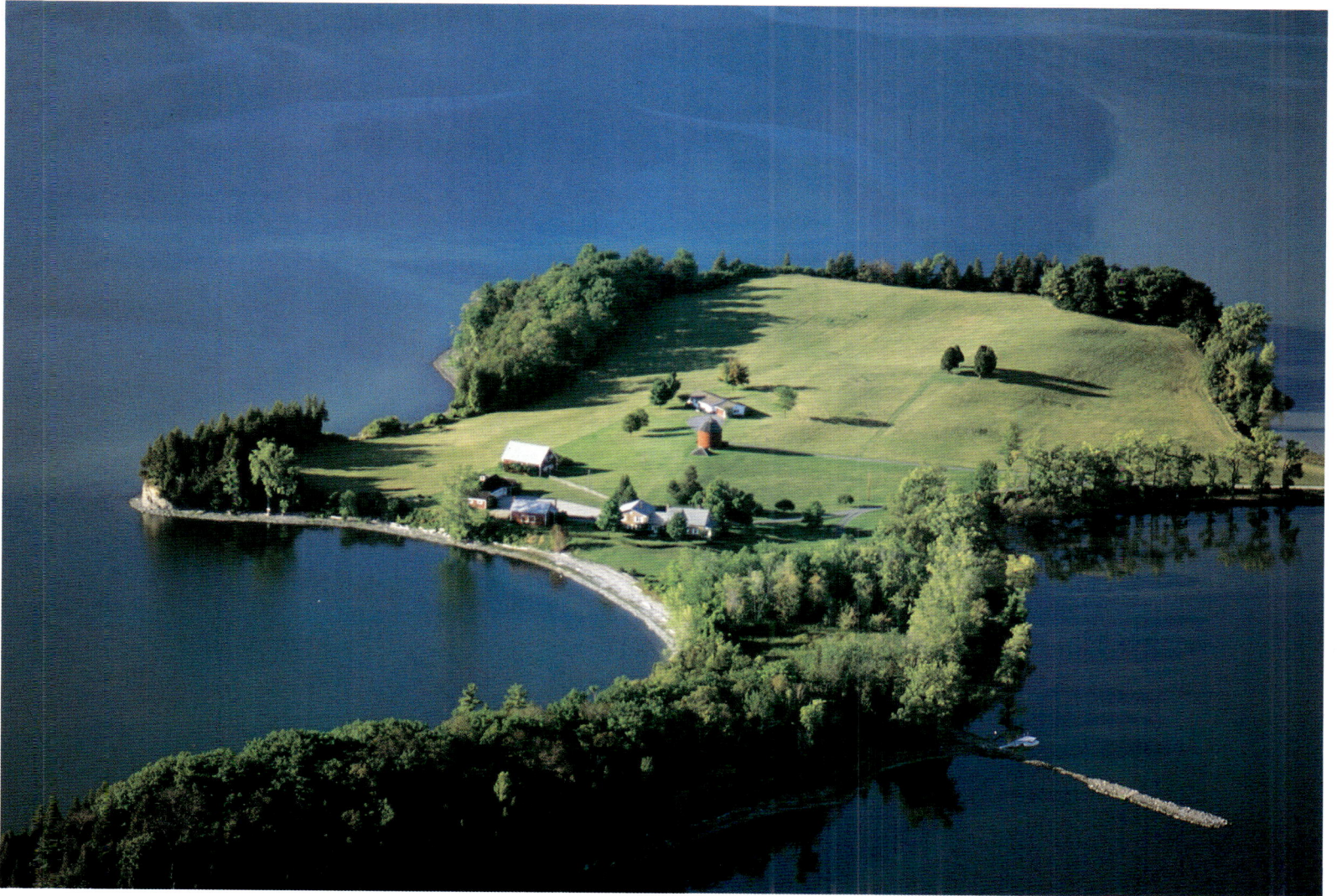

Shelburne Farms once incorporated over 4,000 acres, including a gatekeeper's house, several barns, and houses for farm employees *(above)*. Today the property—reduced to 1,000 acres—is an educational center and museum.

Frederick Law Olmsted, who designed Central Park and the Capitol grounds in Washington, also helped shape the velvet grounds of Shelburne Farms along the shores of Lake Champlain. The "farm" was built in the 1890s by railroad magnate Samuel Webb and his wife, Lila Vanderbilt. The 110-room "farmhouse" *(foreground)* is now operated as an inn.

*T*he shining golden dome of Montpelier's State House is visible for miles around. With a population of about 8,200, Montpelier is the smallest state capital in the country. Its idyllic setting in the Green Mountains along the Winooski River makes up for in scenery what it lacks in size. Jacob Davis (a Francophile) settled and named the town in 1788; it has been the capital since 1805.

Of the 114 or so covered bridges in Vermont, few can compare with the 460-foot-long Windsor-Cornish Bridge. It is the longest in the country, spanning the Connecticut River between Windsor (Vermont) and Cornish (New Hampshire). Of course, if you are in New Hampshire the bridge is referred to as the Cornish-Windsor Bridge.

The "snow of Stowe" is famous across the Northeast. Over 50 ski lodges dot the steep slopes of Mount Mansfield, giving the town a decidedly festive atmosphere. The Community Church provides the proper New England touch. Behind the church, a recreation path (constructed in the 1980s) climbs the mountain road, providing a pedestrian way through one of America's most exquisite villages.

Where the pavement ends and the gravel roads begin, a world of funky homesteads like this one on Podunk Brook, near West Hartford, awaits adventurous travelers. The West Hartford area also has the honor of being the birthplace of Horace Wells, who discovered laughing gas.

A different mood pervades the country-side around Woodstock, which was settled by wealthy intellectuals in 1761. Nearby, the Ottauquechee River *(right)* flows through scenery that is heartbreakingly lovely. "It beats a day on the Woodstock green" (a quote from Vermont poet Daniel L. Cady) was once a phrase describing the pinnacle of pleasure.

212

Streams of winter-morning light awaken
the 10,000 students at UVM in Burlington.
Universitas Viridis Montis (University
Green Mountains) is a stately name for a
stately university that boasts buildings by
America's finest architects.

After working all day in granite quarries, stonecutters in Barre seem to prefer wooden houses for their rest, like these rambling homes near the quarries. Largely of Scottish and Italian descent, the stonecutters of Barre have a reputation as a passionate and fun-loving group, in contrast to their more genteel Vermont neighbors.

Near Hartford, a row of dairy farms rolls toward the horizon of the Green Mountains. Though Vermont means "mountains" to most visitors, the heart and soul of the state remains on the farm. Vermont at last count had the third-smallest population among the 50 states. More than half of all Vermonters live in towns with fewer than 2,500 people, which makes Vermont in an overall sense the most rural state in America.

THE GRANITE SPINE

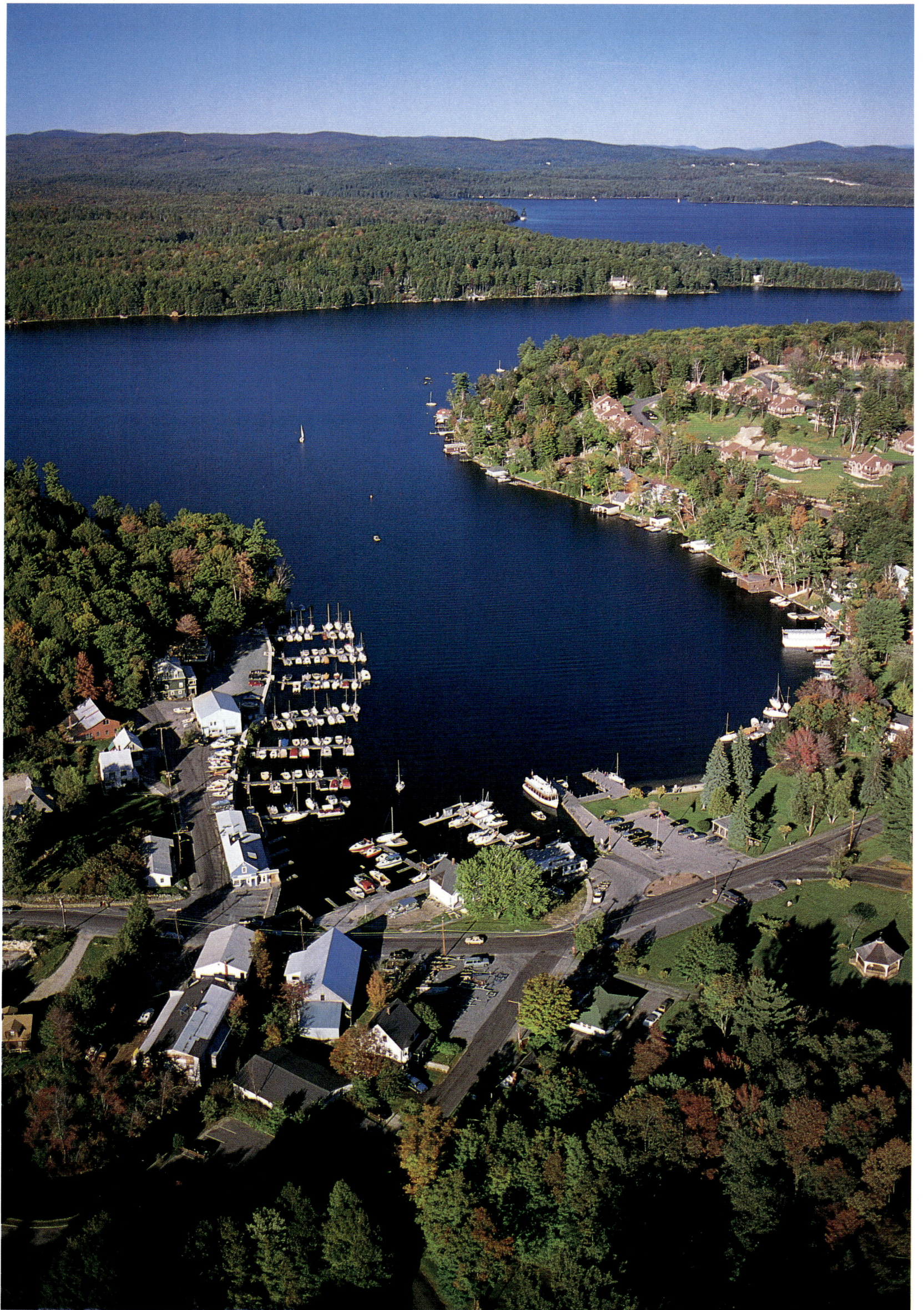

"It is restful," Robert Frost once wrote, "just to think about New Hampshire." Sugar orchards and deserted old farms, October's radiant maples and birches, crystalline winter mornings and luminous lakeside sunsets were likely on the great New England poet's mind. Or one might think of the Shaker community at Canterbury, where in the nineteenth century as many as 300 souls pledged themselves to communal living, celibacy and emulation of Christ's simple life. They would leave a legacy of what may well be the most wondrously simple, inventive and beautiful craftsmanship ever achieved in America.

There is also majestic, mountained New Hampshire: the summit of Mount Washington, at 6,288 feet northeastern America's highest peak, where on April 12, 1934, the wind velocity was 231 miles per hour—the highest ever recorded; the granite face of the Old Man of the Mountains, and the splendid network of foot trails connecting all the White Mountains; the Kancamagus Wilderness Highway, 34 miles of pristine mountain- and streamscape, protected from all tourist-trade tackiness; the great intermountain "notches"— Pinkham, Crawford, Franconia—where the glaciers kindly left place for humans to struggle through; and superb secondary ranges like the Sandwich, where noble Mount Chocorua, topped by a pyramidal white granite cone, looks down on two picturesque small lakes.

Off to the southwest, rising in lonely splendor, is Mount Monadnock, beloved of Thoreau and Emerson and countless other nineteenth-century writers and artists. To the west, the Connecticut River Valley and Hanover, home of Dartmouth College. And in center state, the region of the Great Ponds of New Hampshire—mighty Winnipesaukee with its 365 wooded islands, crystal-clear Newfound, Squam, Sunapee, Ossipie and their smaller cousins.

Hikers, skiers, boaters, gawking tourists enjoy it all—indeed so much that "condo-mania," roaring boat madness and snowmobiling have produced some true environmental challenges. But what twentieth-century visitors rarely sense is the daunting side of this state's history.

Left: Lake Sunapee is a popular resort area in all seasons.
Previous pages: Highest post in the land: New Hampshire's Presidential Range.

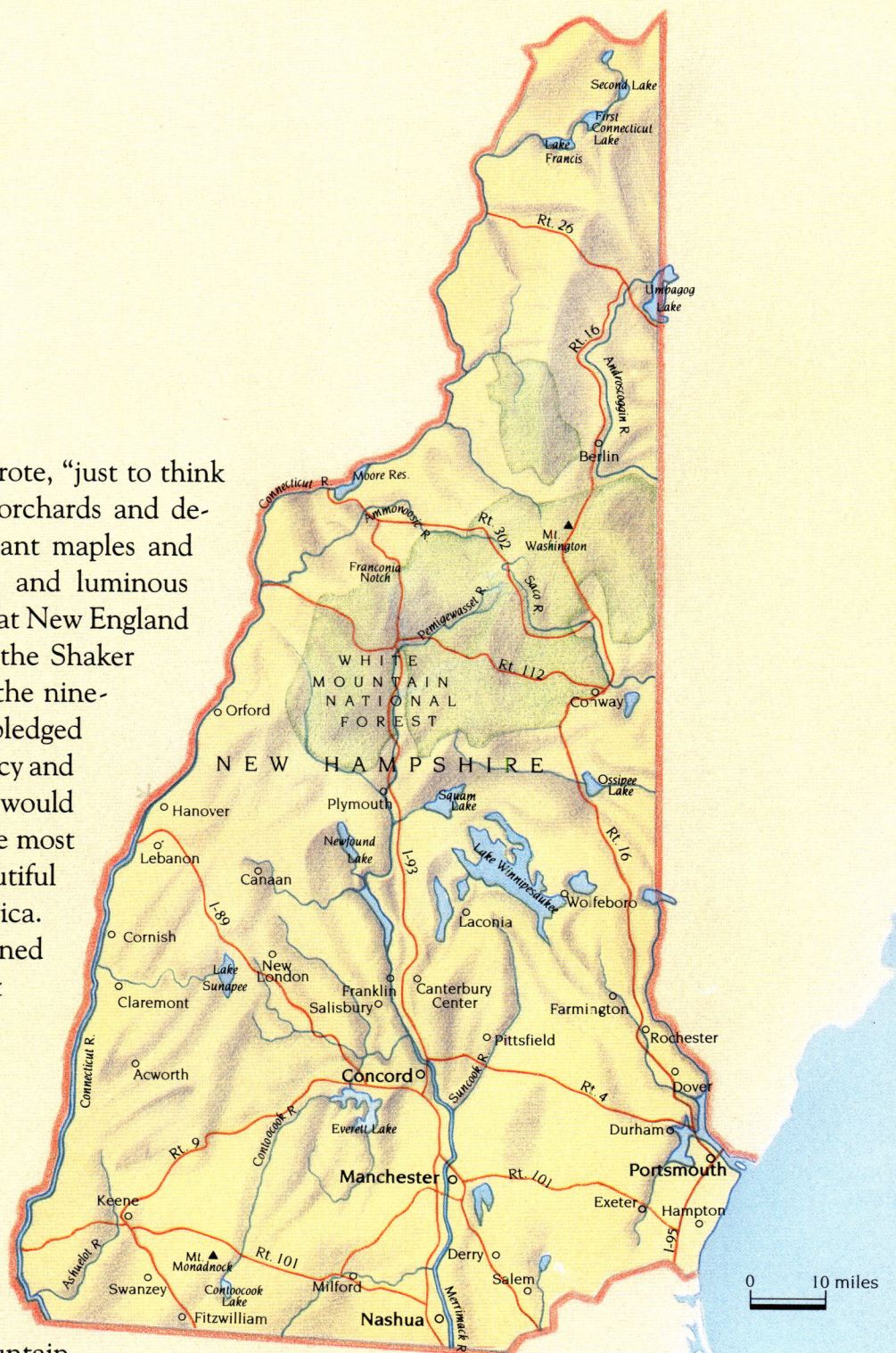

The old Shaker saying "It's a gift to be simple" finds expression in the Shaker community of Canterbury (above), established in 1776 by two followers of Shaker founder Mother Ann Lee. Another Shaker woman, Sister Tabitha Babbitt, invented the circular saw, which no doubt came in handy for the 1902 construction of the Mount Washington Hotel (right), said to be the largest wooden building in the state.

The first European settlers in New Hampshire indeed had reason to believe they'd been dealt a lean hand. The granite-strewn soil was so meager that it was said the pioneers had to "pry the sun up with a crowbar." There were few fertile valleys to encourage a rich agriculture like Vermont's. The state's window to the sea was but eighteen miles, precluding the plentiful harvests Maine took from the Atlantic.

Nor was New Hampshire's political birth salubrious. Powerful royal grantees and colonial governors hurried to grab immense tracts of land for their personal possession. Their greed generated a deep popular suspicion of leaders and government which

lingers to this day in the form of ferocious opposition to taxes and activist government programs.

Up in the "North Country" toward the Canadian border, lumbering moved in; the region is still a raw, rather distant empire of the woodsman, hunter and backcountry guide. In southern and central New Hampshire, the hillsides were painstakingly cleared by the early farmers. Then, in the mid-1800s, vast numbers of farm families went west, and the fields reverted to forest. Anyone who glorifies the "good old days" should visit an old mountain graveyard near our New Hampshire home. Lined up beside the headstones of Charles Adams and his wife Melinda, who

lived to ripe old ages, are the graves of their three daughters and three 'sons, all of whom died between eleven months and twenty years of age.

The Industrial Revolution came early as textile mills sprang up beside the Merrimack and other rivers racing down the state's tight valleys. The great Amoskeag Manufacturing Company at Manchester became the colossus of the textile world, covering eight million square feet of factory space and hiring 17,000 workers at its zenith. Displaced Yankees provided the first manpower; then, because they deemed it too scarce or too expensive, the mill owners drove wagons up to Quebec to fetch whole families of desperately poor French Canadians—people who would bring their own parish culture, language and customs into an alien, often hostile Puritan environment. The French Canadians would find it tougher to adapt than the Irish—who began arriving before the Civil War, often to work on the railroads—or the Poles, Greeks, Portuguese and Italians who followed later.

The mill owners used child labor, paid miserable wages and fought unions with a vengeance. But they made New Hampshire into a significantly urban and ethnic state, and no one could challenge them until, in the 1920s and 1930s, they were undercut by still cheaper labor in Dixie and driven south, or out of business altogether.

Startling change, reversing the state's economic fate, came after World War II. A phenomenal flow of high-technology-related manufacturing started to pour into New Hampshire's southern reaches, partly because Massachusetts's high-tech-driven Route 128 corridor was but a few miles distant, and partly because New Hampshire offered a pro-business climate of low taxes, low wages and few unions. Suddenly the state of granite and forbidding old mill buildings became one of America's high-tech centers. And southern New Hampshire was transformed from a land of small villages into a vast, sprawling suburban landscape of housing tracts, low-rise factories, shopping malls, sign-laden strip commercial highways and mounting commuter-hour traffic tie-ups.

The avalanche of growth has made New Hampshire the hottest boom state east of Nevada and north

*H*arvest season near Derry brings residents out to the local pumpkin patch to choose the perfect would-be jack-o'-lantern, while apple orchards next door offer U-Pick-Em specials on the forbidden fruit.

*S*et in the woodlands of Lake Sunapee, the Hemphill Power and Light Company operates this small generating plant at Georges Mills. Electricity is generated from burning woodchips leftover from logging and milling operations. Several similiar plants have opened in the state in recent years.

of the Mason-Dixon line. In many years the state has had the lowest unemployment in the entire United States. And its population has been growing at a dizzying rate, from 491,000 on the eve of World War II to a projected 1,333,000 by the year 2000—an increase of *171 percent.*

The state's first-in-the-nation presidential primary brings Hampshirites into the national news every four years, as does the militant conservatism of its leading newspaper, the *Manchester Union Leader.* Aversion to taxes and government remain extreme: New Hampshire has never had a general income or sales tax. (Much income is garnered from "sin taxes" on inexpensive liquor sold to travelers at state-run stores astride the freeways, and from proceeds from America's first twentieth-century state lottery, inaugurated in 1964.)

New Hampshire has had strong environmental organizations since the ultimately successful fight to save the great forest lands around Mount Washington from rapacious cutting and to create a national forest there in 1911. Yet in several critical areas, land-use controls among them, the state's environmental laws have lagged far behind those of Maine and Vermont. And bitter controversy surrounded the building and firing up of the massive nuclear power plant at Seabrook, on the seafront.

Controversy, however, is nothing new to New Hampshire. The state's pugnacious motto is "Live Free or Die." The odd juxtaposition between exhilarating high mountains and burnished lakes on the one hand, and schoolyard-like political brawls on the other, is New Hampshire's history, trademark—and likely future.

The Seabrook Nuclear Power Plant *(above)*, on the New Hampshire coast, received approval for operation in 1990 after an eighteen-year controversy, fought in part over the plant's proximity to Boston, 45 miles south. Nothing of such grave concern touches the postcard village of Canaan *(right)*, on the banks of Canaan Street Lake in western New Hampshire.

The rapid growth of the high-tech industry in southern New Hampshire gave rise to housing developments like this one near Derry. Though the working climate in America has improved since the great factory days, these homes still exhibit a somewhat stark demeanor.

The buildings of the Amoskeag Manufacturing Company stretch, like great looms of memory, for a mile along the banks of the Merrimack River in Manchester. To the Abenaki Indians, *Amoskeag* meant "ancient gathering place." From 1805 to 1936 thousands of anonymous lives gathered at the great factory looms and produced more than four million yards of cloth per week—enough to stretch from New Hampshire to the Rockies.

Ambitious climbers scale the wrinkled
face of Mount Monadnock in southern New
Hampshire, said to be one of the world's most
often climbed mountains. More than 100,000
people reach the 3,165-foot peak each year.
Rising from the countryside of Cheshire
County, the mountain has been a landmark
for generations. *Monadnock* is a general term
for mountains like this one—singular rock
outcroppings that have survived the erosive
forces of wind and rain to rise unaccompanied
above the land.

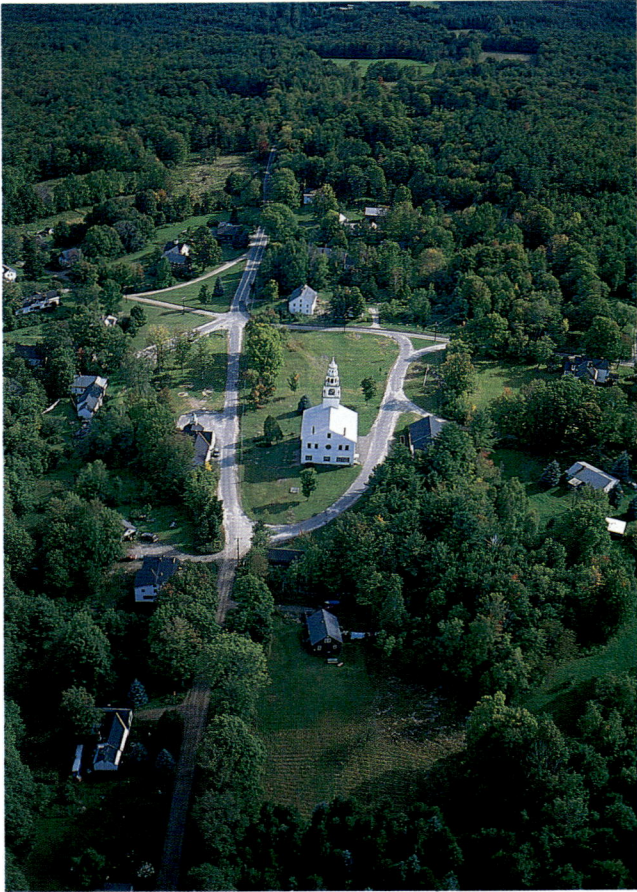

The United Church of Acworth stands patiently watching its tiny village while the seasons circle around it. Some 169 winters, summers, springs and autumns, and 8,788 Sundays, have come and gone since the church was built in 1821. Six generations of children have had time to play on the green and grow up in Acworth.

The red roof of the Swanzey-West Swanzey covered bridge brightens the countryside around the Ashuelot River in southern New Hampshire. The $523.27 spent to build the bridge in 1832 seems to have been a sound investment, even by Yankee standards.

Slimmed down from interstate to parkway, the main north-south route follows the Pemigewasset River through Franconia Notch in the White Mountains. Carved by glaciers during the last Ice Age, "The Notch" and other passages through the White Mountains boast a grandeur more akin to the great scenery of the West. The shaved rows on the side of Cannon Mountain are busy ski slopes come winter. In summer and fall an aerial tramway hoists visitors from the parking lot, 2,100 feet to the top. From there, wide expanses of folded hillsides softened by the golden blush of oak leaves (*right*) are part of the spectacular panorama.

The remains of the ice-sculpting contest from the annual Winter Carnival are still visible on the green of Dartmouth College in Hanover *(left)*. Classes began at Dartmouth in 1770 and, as alumnus Daniel Webster said, "It is a small college and yet there are those who love it."

Members of the Lakes Region Ice Racing Club spend their winter weekends on Berry Pond in Moultonborough *(right)*.

Following pages: In the northern city of Berlin, heaps of woodchips wait to be turned into paper beneath the steaming stacks of the James River Corporation on the Androscoggin River. Berlin, a mill town since its founding in 1825, has much in common with the lumber towns of Maine, just eight miles to the west.

The standard definition of a field is "an open cultivated expanse of land, free from woods, usually devoted to one crop." The farmer who created this masterpiece in the Connecticut River Valley failed on several accounts, but aesthetically his design supercedes all judgments.

When the Puritans arrived in Portsmouth
in 1630, the banks of the Piscataqua River
were covered with wild strawberries. They
called the settlement Strawbery Banke
(*above*) and around it the city of Portsmouth grew. Once neglected, the area is
now an outdoor history museum with
restored houses, craft shops and gardens
adjoining waterfront Prescott Park.

New Hampshire's identity as the Granite
State has undergone certain revisions, as
illustrated by this gravel pit near Derry.
Though the granite industry has declined
with modern steel and concrete design, the
rocky ground of the state yields large stores
of sand and gravel which are used in the
manufacture of concrete.

This prismatic vision of Lake Winnipesaukee *(above)* lives up to its Indian name, "Smile of the Great Spirit." The story tells of an Indian in his canoe on the vast lake when dark storm clouds gathered overhead, obscuring his view. Just before nightfall, a ray of sun broke through the clouds and pointed to his village onshore. The same spirit seems to be at work on the Blackwater River near Salisbury *(right)*. Despite the name, the waters here look very blue, set off by a crimson shore of maples.

The Connecticut River Valley, with its
gentle banks of lush farmlands, was for many
eighteenth-century travelers the landscape
that best reflected the prosperity of the New
World—tame, productive, accessible.
Timothy Dwight was inspired by Orford
(*above*) and the surrounding countryside
(*right*) when he wrote in his 1796 *Travels* of
"sprightly towns" and "lofty woods wildly
contrasting with a rich scene of cultivation."

On Lake Winnipesaukee, a flock of speedboats race toward the open waters. The lake is a liquid wilderness stretching for 72 miles through the White Mountain foothills. More than 365 wooded islands hover on the water's blue surface, enclosed by an intricate shoreline 300 miles in length. Visitors have been coming to "Lake Winnie" for more than a hundred years.

As China has its Great Wall, and Christo his running fence, New Hampshire has this high-voltage powerline pathway cut with cold precision across the slopes of the White Mountains in the Lakes Region. From the air, the grandest plans of men seem small in the overall scheme of things.

A colorful kaleidoscope of autumnal forests encroach on the cultivated fields of this farm in Grafton County near Mascoma Lake.

Robert Frost moved to this homestead in Derry (right), purchased for him by his grandfather in 1900, and lived here until 1909. Frost and his family ran a small hen business from the farm, which was turned into a car junkyard in the late 1930s. It is now a national historic landmark.

Whose woods these are I think I know.
His house is in the village though;
He will not see me stopping here
To watch his woods fill up with snow.

("Stopping by Woods on a
Snowy Evening")

Mountain Majesties: The Presidentials

New England's loftiest peaks, according to a nine-teenth-century account, "seem to have received the name of White Mountains from sailors off the coast, to whom they were a landmark and mystery lifting their crowns of brilliant snow against the blue sky from October until June."

At the heart of this great show is the Presidential Range, a world above timberline, ferocious in climate, forever majestic to the eye, sometimes called "the Ridgepole of New England." Story has it that a legendary climber and trailblazer of the early years, Ethan Allen Crawford, stood with seven friends on Washington's summit one day in 1820 and named the Presidential peaks with great cheers and toasts of rum. The names have stuck—not just Mount Washington but companion peaks named then and after for American statesmen: Mount Adams (perhaps the most imposing peak of the entire range), Mount Jefferson, Mount Madison, Mount Monroe, Mount Webster, Mount Jackson and Mount Clay. In the twentieth century onetime Mount Pleasant joined the Presidential constellation, renamed after a New Hampshire favorite, Dwight David Eisenhower.

The 2,000-mile-long Appalachian Trail, stretching from Maine to Georgia, follows the crest of the Presidentials for many miles. These peaks are served by North America's greatest network of foot trails, many the handiwork of the Appalachian Mountain Club. The AMC welcomes the hiker at strategically located high mountain huts such as Lakes of the Clouds, in the saddle between Washington and Monroe. One might, indeed, forget thousands of nights spent in hotels across the world. But never the warmth of welcome, the hot chocolate, the hearty supper and cot for the night at Lakes of the Clouds after a long day's hike. Or awakening at sunrise to see these majestic peaks—sentinels and signature pieces of a region—emerge from the early morning mist.

Monuments of strength and lofty attainment, like the statesmen they were named for, the Presidential Range shines beneath a snowy mantle. Pictured here are Mount Washington, Mount Monroe, Mount Franklin and Mount Eisenhower.

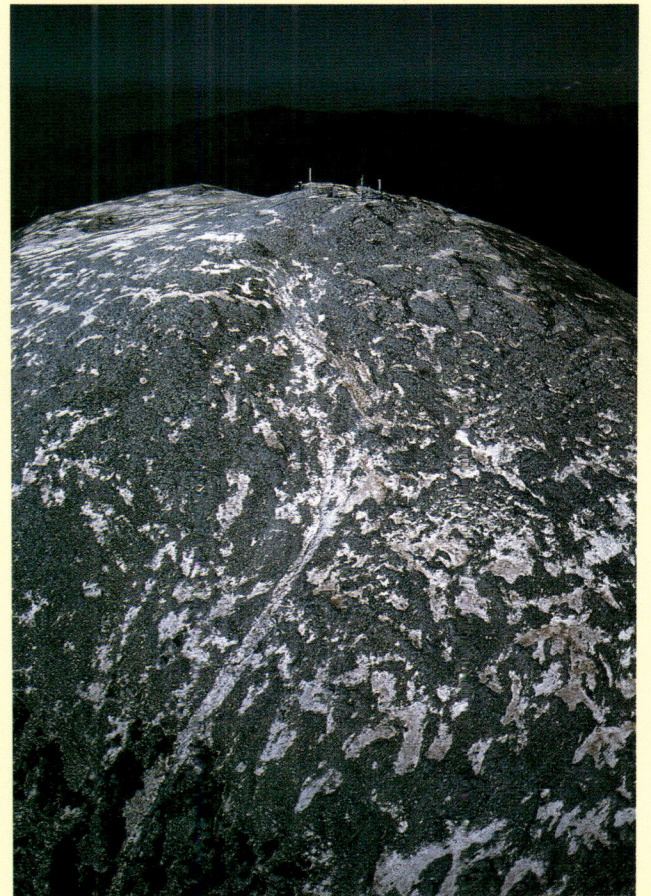

Top: The Mount Washington Cog Railway reaches its final destination after a 1¹/₂-hour ride up the mountain's western ridge. *Above:* Like a small planet in its own galaxy, the stone shoulder of Mount Washington turns toward nightfall.

Sunset over the White Mountains of New Hampshire

ACKNOWLEDGMENTS

The producers of *Over New England* would like to thank the following individuals and institutions for their assistance:

Joan Baumbach; Edward Bennett; Linda Case; Liz Cunningham; Steve Dunwell; Fitchburg Colonial Aviation (Fitchburg, Massachusetts); Sanny Himawan; Hyannis Air Service (Cape Cod); Leslie Jonath; Frank Keefe; Robert Kelly; LADCO (West Lebanon, New Hampshire); Logan Airport Control Tower; George Marsden; Richard Marshall; Metropolitan Boston Transit Authority; Tom Morgan; Michael Newton and John Carver of Broadcast Properties (Boston, Massachusetts); Geraldine A. O'Brien and Michael R. Kramer of New England Telephone (Boston, Massachusetts); Rapid Lasergraphics (San Francisco); Seth Resnick; Carolyn Chick Smith and Natalie R. Cox of Cabot Communications (Boston, Massachusetts); James L. Sullivan, Greater Boston Chamber of Commerce; Wiggins Airways (Norwood, Massachusetts); Chris Wise; Ruth Wise.

THE PROJECT

Like America itself, *Over New England*— both the book and the public television documentary—had their birthdays on the Fourth of July. To get the book literally off the ground, aerial photographer Steve Proehl spent his first day of shooting in the skies above Boston Harbor, following the graceful arcs of the USS *Constitution* as it was turned around in the harbor during the city's Fourth of July celebration.

Exactly a year later, a film crew from Seattle's KCTS Television, comprising producer/director Jeff Gentes and videographer Marc Pingry, circled the same waters, recording the historic scene for the *Over New England* television documentary.

Both book and video crew were equipped with a detailed "shootlist" for each state, compiled by location researchers Richard Marshall and Barbara Roether. These shootlists were augmented by suggestions from author Neal Peirce, as he wrote his text for the book during the fall and winter of 1989–90, alternating between his Washington, D.C., office and his weekend retreat on Newfound Lake, New Hampshire.

"In aerial photography the weather is your master," says veteran aerial photographer Steve Proehl, and videographer Marc Pingry would be the last to disagree.

"Your life revolves around the sun, wind and clouds," adds Proehl, "and New England weather is especially notorious. Most of the country receives its weather from the prevailing westerlies, whereas in the Northeast it's delivered from any one of four directions at any time of the year. That makes planning and scheduling a guessing game at best, but changing light conditions and gathering clouds make for great photo opportunities."

In shooting still photographs, Proehl says that the key is to maintain high shutter speeds in order to minimize the effect of engine vibration. "I also tape my Nikon F4s to 'infinity' — there will be no object at less distance from this platform."

Except for helicopter shoots over Boston and parts of New Hampshire, all of the photography for the book was shot from Cessna 172 Skyhawks, the aircraft of choice for aerial work. In order to avoid reflections, the planes' windows were latched open—an uncomfortable reality when confronted with the freezing temperatures of a New England winter.

For moving images, the helicopter was the preferred platform. The *Over New England* helicopter was provided with both nose and side camera mounts, which allowed videographer Marc Pingry to move around his subject in a gentle arc to establish mood, or to track rapidly across the terrain to add pace and excitement. Television producer/director Jeff Gentes found his aerial role to be different from land-based film direction. "Instead of directing the cameraman, I had to direct the pilot to point the camera in the direction where I wanted Marc to shoot. An experienced pilot, though, quickly develops an almost symbiotic rapport with the videographer, which allowed me to plan the next shot."

New England Telephone: "The Place We Call Home"

The Underwriter

New England Telephone is proud to sponsor *Over New England* because New England is not just the place where we do business; it's the place we call home.

We're part of the fabric of daily life in New England. We live here. We're 25,000 of your neighbors and friends. We share the same values, the same heritage, the same future.

We built New England's telephone system over 100 years ago, and we've always been here when New Englanders needed us for residential and business phone service. Today, New England Telephone continues to pioneer in telephone services for the region, employing state-of-the-art technology to anticipate and satisfy the increasingly sophisticated needs of our customers.

And to help improve our communities in more personal ways, New England Telephone and its people volunteer time and resources in our schools, hospitals, veterans' homes, senior centers and Special Olympics.

All of this is why we're the one for you, New England. And why we're the natural one to underwrite this aerial celebration of New England.

New England Telephone
A **NYNEX** Company

INDEX